Forever Ruined
for the Ordinary

The Adventure of Hearing and
Obeying God's Voice

JOY DAWSON

OLIVER
NELSON™

THOMAS NELSON PUBLISHERS
Nashville

Unless otherwise noted, all scripture references are taken from the NEW KING JAMES VERSION. Copyright © 1979, 1980, 1982 by Thomas Nelson, Inc. Used by permission. All rights reserved.

Scripture marked NIV is taken from the HOLY BIBLE, NEW INTERNATIONAL VERSION. Copyright © 1973, 1978, 1984 International Bible Society. Used by permission of Zondervan Bible Publishers.

Scripture marked RSV is taken from the REVISED STANDARD VERSION OF THE BIBLE, Old Testament Section, Copyright © 1952; New Testament Section, First Edition, Copyright ©1946; Second Edition Copyright © 1971 by Division of Christian Education of the Churches of Christ in the United States of America.

Scripture marked TLB is taken from *The Living Bible*. Copyright © 1971 by Tyndale House Publishers, Wheaton, Illinois. All rights reserved.

Scripture marked KJV is taken from the King James Version of the Bible.

Scripture marked AMP is taken from THE AMPLIFIED BIBLE. Old Testament copyright © 1965, 1987 by the Zondervan Corporation. The Amplified New Testament copyright © 1958, 1987 by the Lockman Foundation. Used by permission.

Scripture marked THE MESSAGE is taken from *The Message*. Copyright © by Eugene H. Peterson, 1993, 1994, 1995, 1996. Used by permission of NavPress Publishing Group.

"The Release of the Spirit through Brokenness" is taken from *Women of Destiny Bible* copyright © 2000, Thomas Nelson, Inc. Used by permission.

Library of Congress Cataloging-in-Publication Data

Dawson, Joy.
    Forever ruined for the ordinary : the adventure of hearing and obeying the voice of God / Joy Dawson.
      p. cm.
    ISBN 0-7852-6682-8
    1. Christian life. I. Title.
    BV4501.2.D3935 2001
    248.4—dc21   2001030126
                                             CIP

Printed in the United States of America

4 5 6 BVG 06 05 04 03 02 01

Contents

Contents

Section 6:

Section 7:

Appendix A:

Appendix B:

Appendix C:

Appendix D:

Dedication

To my precious family, who are my closest friends
and treasured gifts from God.

My husband, Jim

My son, John, and daughter-in-love, Julie
Grandchildren David and his wife Katiucia,
Paul, Matthew, and Rachel Dawson

My daughter, Jill, and son-in-love John Bills
Grandchildren Jenny and Justin Bills

My prayer is that they all will completely fulfill
their destinies by increasingly hearing and obeying
God's voice.

Acknowledgments

*W*ithout the constant enabling power of the Holy Spirit, this book would never have been written. He inspired, directed, and energized me all the way through. Therefore *all* the glory must go to God for the ways in which He will use the contents.

My beloved husband and lifelong best friend, Jim, and I have worked on this project together. With God's enablement Jim has done all the word processing on the computer. His prayers, patient listening, and wise responses have also been invaluable.

I am deeply indebted and grateful to those intercessor friends who diligently prayed us through. I was very conscious that God was answering their many prayers.

It was a delight to work with Victor Oliver, Beth Clark, Cindy Blades, and Pamela Clements of Thomas Nelson Publishers. They are a great team; so cooperative and sensitive to this author's needs, which is greatly appreciated.

JOY DAWSON

Section

1

Everyone's Privilege

Have you ever said, "If only I could hear God's voice, I would do whatever He told me"? Many years ago, that's exactly what I said. Apparently that statement got God's attention, because as soon as I started to get still enough and quiet enough to listen, He started to speak to me specifically, personally, and conversationally in a whole new dimension. My relationship with God became exciting and infinitely more meaningful. I was tuned in and turned on to God, the Creator and Sustainer of the universe. I took off on the adventure of a lifetime—hearing and obeying God's voice. I was forever ruined for the ordinary.

Our God is the most extraordinary, fascinating, intriguing, exciting, mysterious, yet accessible Being in the universe. It still boggles my mind and excites my heart that the One who has the power to speak worlds and planets into existence and uphold them by the word of His power delights to tell me where my lost pen, needle, button, or ten cents is located. I'm totally impressed by His commitment to be personally involved with the creatures He has created.

"Aw, c'mon, get real," you may say. "You mean the Almighty God has actually spoken to you and told you where your lost pen was located?" Sure He has.

I had given my mother a pretty blue pen and a tapestry case. When she died, I acquired it. It became my favorite pen because it was so smooth-flowing; it was the perfect size and color; and besides, it had belonged to someone very precious to me, so it had sentimental value.

One day at my office I noticed it was missing, so I looked everywhere I knew and asked God to help me find it. My husband and secretary joined in the search, but it never showed up. Finally I said to God, "In Your omniscience, You know exactly where it is and because of Your understanding love, I believe You see it is important to me to find it, so please tell me exactly where it is." I stopped and listened. Immediately an impression came into my mind in sentence form, "It's in the office bathroom."

I had looked carefully in the bathroom earlier and had seen nothing. It seemed the most unlikely place. But I have learned to obey that voice. I looked again. I then saw it on the floor in an obscure place, behind the toilet! Only God knows how it got there, and only He could help me find it. At times like this I worship Him for His humility to be involved in my little world.

The more we fulfill the Biblical conditions of hearing God's voice—take the lid off the limitations we impose on the ways He speaks—we will prove Him to be anything but a big cosmic power hovering over the universe, disinterestedly detached from the details of the lives He brought into existence. That's not the God I write about in this book. No sir! No ma'am!

When we are born again at conversion through commitment of our lives to the Lord Jesus (see Appendix A) and enter into a relationship with God as our Father, we have every reason to expect Him to speak to us. Have you ever noticed that the most natural thing a parent does is to initiate communication, and in time, conversation with his or her child? It was our heavenly Father's idea in the first place to talk to us and listen to us because He created us for intimate friendship with Himself. And fellowship requires a two-way conversation. It does not happen without at least two participants. It's that simple.

So aren't you glad that normal Christianity includes your hearing your heavenly Father's voice any time He sees that you have a need? I have always been puzzled by well-meaning good Christian people who would say that those of us who hear God's voice at a personal level today, apart from through His Word, are weird. I think it weird if we do not expect to hear and experience hearing His voice as a way of life and in the many ways He has chosen to communicate with us. After all, Jesus said that His sheep hear His voice, know His voice, and follow Him (John 10:3–4, 27). But then again, sheep are simple and uncomplicated. So I figure that those who remain childlike and trusting, believing that it's primarily the Shepherd's responsibility to make the signals clear enough for the sheep to know which pasture they're to be in, will keep their eyes on the Shepherd, hear His voice, and go in the right direction without a lot of stress.

Although I have lived in California since 1971, I originated in New Zealand where there are many millions more sheep than people. I never cease to be intrigued when I see the incredibly close interaction between the shepherds and highly trained sheepdogs. These extremely intelligent animals never take their eyes off the shepherd, are totally obedient to his signals, and never move independently of him. But the moment the shepherd gives a specific kind of whistle if the sheep are not going in the right direction, the dogs tear into action, barking and rounding up the sheep, helping them make it, but never harming them.

How like the Holy Spirit. If we really want to do God's will, and because we do not fully understand how to find it and may be heading in the wrong direction, we can trust our heavenly Shepherd to send the Holy Spirit to give us strong warning signals to steer us in the right direction. That should comfort all of us and help us to relax.

God has a detailed, remarkable plan for every person's life—a plan consistent with His character. He is a remarkable God. But He never intended us to make our plans and then ask Him to bless them. What an insult to the One who created us and who alone knows how to fulfill us.

We read in Jeremiah 10:23, "I know, O LORD, that a man's life is not his own; it is not for man to direct his steps" (NIV). Okay, so obviously, in order for us to know what His plans for our lives are, we must be able to hear His voice. The good news is that "A man's steps are directed by the LORD. / How then can anyone understand His own way?" (Proverbs 20:24 NIV).

We don't have the faintest idea what is best for us, so what a relief that there is a Master Mind who does—a God with a heart full of unfathomable love and with the ability to communicate with all of us who want to listen and obey. That gives cause for rejoicing and more relaxing.

Jesus said, "Man shall not live by bread alone, but by every word that proceeds from the mouth of God" (Matthew 4:4). All this adds up to the fact that it is totally impossible to effectively function as a Christian without hearing God's voice as a way of life. The reassuring news is that "He who is of God hears God's words" (John 8:47) and, "Everyone who is of the truth hears My voice" (John 18:37).

That last promise tells us that if we'll be 100 percent honest with God, He will make His voice crystal clear to us. Can we say, "I'll buy that. That's a fair deal"? I can assure you it is a fabulous deal. It pays dividends every time.

However, if our main concept of God and ourselves is that of a Master and His servants, we will only expect Him to give orders about what we consider to be important issues. This wrong concept doesn't match with the longing in God's heart for intimacy of relationship with us. We, in turn, deprive ourselves of experiencing true fulfillment.

Remember, one of the main reasons God made us in His image and likeness is so that we can interact with Him. I believe part of God's unparalleled greatness is His desire and ability to be intimately involved in the smallest details of the lives of billions of the creatures He created and to be communicating to them all at one time, if necessary, in precisely the way and timing that serve their best interests—and in their native language. Mind-boggling to say the least! It is totally outside our ability to comprehend *how* God does this because we are finite, but it is within our ability to accept the fact that He *does*. Why? Because we are talking about the One with the ultimate gifting in communication skills, who is at the same time the ultimate Lover of our souls. We pause to wonder in awe, in worship, and in gratitude.

Here is how it works. A pastor friend of mine was driving me to speak at a pastors' conference at a retreat center outside of a city in northern California. He asked me if I would share with him how to better hear the voice of God. I was in the process of doing so when he said, "I'm sorry to have to interrupt you, but I'm not sure we're taking the right directions and I feel so responsible to get you to the meeting on time."

I immediately said, "Fine, just pull over to a suitable place on the highway and we'll put this teaching into operation. God will soon tell you. It's not complicated."

I briefly reiterated the need and how to eliminate the only two other sources that could bring impressions to his mind other than God. (We can have impressions from our own thoughts and from satanic influences, and I elaborate on those impressions later in this book.) I then encouraged him to ask God the simple question for which he needed an answer. I assured him I would be praying for him while he fulfilled the conditions of hearing God's voice, and then listened to Him. After a few minutes, I looked over at him and saw that he was uptight and straining.

As diplomatically and gently as I knew how, I suggested that he picture himself as a little boy of three, climbing up on his Father God's knee, resting his head on his Father's chest, and just relaxing and saying, "Thanks, Daddy, for the answer"—with no more asking. The pastor said, "You know, I'm not much good at all this, but I'll give it a go. You see, Joy, I've always related to God as I did to my natural father. I only asked my dad about the major decisions; all the little everyday stuff I talked over with my mother. So I figure that we shouldn't bother God with this kind of thing."

I thanked him for his honesty, but explained that as males and females we are all made in the likeness and image of God (see Genesis 1:26–27). Therefore God has to have equal components of male and female within His Being. I also said that as God is love and yearns to have an intimate relationship with every one of us, this quality of love excludes no circumstances in our lives. The pastor saw the logic of all this and said, "Okay, I'll do as you suggest."

Within a few minutes, I heard the pastor chuckling quietly, and then he said, "I heard God's voice. A clear impression in the form of words, 'Son, you're on the right road,' came into my mind." We laughed and thanked God together and continued driving. About ten or fifteen minutes later he laughed again and said, "I've just seen a sign confirming that we're on the right road." That should not be surprising in the light of the following two promises: "The LORD will guide you continually" (Isaiah 58:11) and "He will be our guide even to death" (Psalm 48:14). That covers the small circumstances as well as the big.

We read in Genesis 5:24 that "Enoch walked with God; and he was not, for God took him." That does not mean that Enoch spent his life on another planet, disassociated from other people. It simply means that he had a closer relationship with God than others, and is a perfect picture of what normal Christianity should be.

My life's motto is, "To know God and make Him known." The outcome of knowing God intimately should be a deep desire for others to experience the same wonderful fulfillment. The following story illustrates how this adventure works in the everyday circumstances of life.

My husband, Jim, and I were out on a morning prayer walk in Johannesburg, South Africa. I was speaking at conferences in that nation. We were interceding for others as we were passing a large B.M.W. car assembly plant where a guard was on duty in a guard house at the entrance. I had an impression that I was to stop and speak to the man about spiritual things. Instantly I knew that impression came from the Holy Spirit. For decades, God has used this method to let me know I am to witness to someone about the reality of the Lord Jesus Christ.

As I obeyed this prompting and walked over to the high fence surrounding this facility, the understanding came for the right approach. "Good morning, sir. My husband and I are out on a walk praying for this nation, and I felt impressed to ask you if you knew the Lord Jesus Christ personally."

"No, I don't, but I've been thinking a lot about that lately," was his sincere, warm, respectful response.

"Well, would you like me to tell you how you can know Him personally?"

"Yes, please."

Jim stood by, silently praying, while in the next seven to ten minutes I explained the implications related to committing his life to Christ. After the man indicated that he understood clearly and was ready to do so, I led him responsively through a prayer of commitment, thoroughly covering each step. We left him with the promise that we would be back at the same time the next morning with a pamphlet I had written that covered what I had shared and contained the prayer that he had just prayed (See Appendix A). I asked him if he knew of a good church that he could attend in this area, and he said, "No." I prayed that God would help him find the right one, and we continued on our prayer walk, rejoicing.

The next morning as we were out prayer walking again, a

man came jogging from behind us and passed us. The Holy Spirit impressed upon my spirit that I was to speak to him, and I had to run to catch up with him.

I said, "Excuse me, sir, do you know the Lord Jesus personally?"

He stopped. With a big smile, he said, "I sure do."

"That's fabulous," I said. "You're just the person I need."

I explained what had happened the previous morning and asked my newfound brother in Christ if he could recommend the right church for the newly converted guard at the B.M.W. plant to attend. "Sure can," was the immediate response. It so happened that the whole conversation took place very near the gate of the B.M.W. plant, so we soon introduced the jogging Christian to the new convert. He was overjoyed to see us and to be given the recommendation and directions to a vital church in his area. I then went over the points on my pamphlet of what it takes to maintain the Christian life, and prayed with him.

There is a lot to learn in this school of intimate friendship with God, but it is not complicated. Even children can, and do, experience it.

My granddaughter, Jenny Bills, shares one of her many experiences of hearing God's voice.

When I was fourteen years old, I needed to have my wisdom teeth removed in order to make way for my other teeth to move properly in my braces. I was very afraid of having needles put into me. I had no cavities, and had never had surgery, so when I was told that my wisdom teeth had to be pulled I was really scared, to the point that I would shake and cry.

8:00 A.M. was the time on the day scheduled for my teeth to be removed. At 6:00 A.M. I was very afraid and cried out to God for His help. He answered me by speaking the words into my mind, "Psalm forty-six, verse five." When I looked it up in my Bible it said, "God is within her, she will not fall; God will help her at break of day" (NIV).

Immediately all fear left, God's peace filled my heart and I was able to walk into the doctor's rooms singing worship songs. It blew me away that God would even speak to me from His Word about the exact timing for which I needed to have His reassuring comfort: "at break of day." And even the references were to "her" and "she." What a personal, caring God. He's so real.

Our daughter Jill shares one of the many stories she and her family have experienced in relation to seeking God for directions.

Our daughter Jenny was happy in her private Christian school experience until she attended her first year of junior high school. The teachers were mature Christians, and the curriculum was Bible-based, yet many of the children she had grown up with were turning from their Christian values and becoming more influenced by the godless culture. Jenny began to express to us her concerns for her own walk with God and asked us to consider homeschooling her in order for her to stay spiritually strong. At that time I had been a substitute teacher in her school, so the consideration was not too unrealistic.

This decision was something her dad and I felt was one

in which Jenny should hear directly from God. It was such a lifestyle-altering decision. Jenny went into her bedroom, poured out her heart before the Lord, and sought Him diligently to speak to her. She came to us with a strong conviction in her spirit that homeschooling was for her. Her dad and I also sought the Lord together with her, and received the same deep conviction and peace that this was His will. Jenny completed high school at home, and then began training to be a missionary in Youth With A Mission (YWAM).

In the next section, we will get very practical and look at the conditions God requires us to fulfill in order for this intimate relationship with Him to work.

Section

2

Conditions for Hearing God's Voice

Humility

One of our greatest universal needs is to experience and walk in humility at increasingly deeper levels. Period. When it comes to experiencing divine guidance, the Bible makes it clear that we will not make any progress without it. "He guides the humble in what is right and teaches them His way" (Psalm 25:9 NIV). Pride feels no need to inquire of God and take time to seek His face. When we see this from God's perspective, it is both proud and foolish to live independently of Him by continuously making our own decisions and hoping or presuming they are in His will. The Bible says that "God looks down from heaven upon the sons of men, To see if there are any that are wise, that seek after God" (Psalm 53:2 RSV).

After David made the mistake and experienced the subsequent horrible implications of not seeking God for direction, he cried out to God, "Keep back Your servant also from presumptuous sins; let them not have dominion over me. Then I shall be blameless, and I shall be innocent of great transgression" (Psalm 19:13).

Only the Holy Spirit can reveal to us that presumption in God's sight is "great transgression," based in pride. We have a further insight into God's perspective on this subject from

Zephaniah 1:6: "Those who have turned back from following the LORD, and have not sought the LORD, nor inquired of Him." God calls the lack of inquiry of Him, "backsliding." You may be thinking, *Well, I seek God on all the major issues, but I don't bother Him with the little decisions.* Oh really? It was just as important to Jesus, who modeled humility for us, to seek God the Father's face related to matters large or small. He said, "I tell you the truth, the Son can do nothing by Himself; He can do only what He sees His Father doing, because whatever the Father does the Son also does" (John 5:19 NIV). Have you noticed that this level of humility and dependence produced incredible results?

Faith

Faith is the second condition necessary for hearing God's voice. We have to believe God will speak to us. Hebrews 11:6 makes that starkly clear: "Without faith it is impossible to please Him, for he who comes to God must believe that He is, and that He is a rewarder of those who diligently seek Him." By far the most important basis for our faith is the character of God. Let's look at some of His characteristics.

- As a God of the knowledge of all that is knowable, He has the answers. He knows where He wants us to be, at what time, and what we are to say and do.

- As a God of limitless power, He has the ability to communicate in every language.

• As a God of infinite wisdom, He knows how and when to communicate.

• As a God of total justice, He will only tell us to do what is right and just for us and everyone else involved with our decisions.

• As a God of absolute righteousness, He will never tell us to do anything unholy or inconsistent with His character or the principles in His Word, the Bible.

• As a God of unfathomable love, He longs to communicate with us.

One of the most comforting and encouraging Bible verses I know backs this up: "Yes, He loves the people; all His saints are in Your hand; they sit down at Your feet; everyone receives Your words" (Deuteronomy 33:3). The NIV says, ". . . and from You [they] receive instruction." If you are wondering whether you qualify for God to care enough about your need to hear His voice, listen to this verse: "In Your unfailing love You will lead the people You have redeemed" (Exodus 15:13 NIV).

Now we really do not need anything more than the knowledge of God's character to believe that He will guide us, but as an added bonus He has given us promises from His Word. The following verses are fuel to further feed the fire of our faith:

• "I will instruct you and teach you in the way you should go; I will guide you with My eye" (Psalm 32:8).

- "For this is God, our God forever and ever; He will be our guide even to death" (Psalm 48:14).

- "Your ears shall hear a word behind you, saying, 'This is the way, walk in it,' whenever you turn to the right hand or whenever you turn to the left" (Isaiah 30:21).

- "Thus says the LORD, your Redeemer, the Holy One of Israel: 'I am the LORD your God, who teaches you to profit, who leads you by the way you should go" (Isaiah 48:17).

A Clean Heart

The third condition to ensure that we will hear God's voice, is the need for us to have a clean heart. "If I regard iniquity in my heart, the Lord will not hear" (Psalm 66:18). We need to get quiet and give God time to convict us if necessary.

At one time I was desperate for direction from God to know whether or not I was to accept an invitation to speak at a conference, having sought Him for days without receiving an answer. The people inviting me had phoned saying they had to have an answer that day. As soon as I asked God if there was unconfessed sin in my life, He convicted me of a bad attitude I had had toward someone. Upon repenting and making restitution, the guidance was immediately released.

The truth of Proverbs 8:20 was made more clear to me that day. "I lead in the way of righteousness, in the midst of the paths of judgment" (KJV).

God's silences can at times be attributed to undealt-with sin in our lives. For example, when the Scribes were not prepared to be honest with Jesus, He refused to answer their questions (see Luke 20:1–8).

A Yielded Will

The fourth condition in order to hear God's voice is having a yielded will. It is important to understand that guidance from God will be according to the extent of our commitment to do His will. God, in the enormity of His grace, will always work with whatever we give Him. In other words, if we say we will serve Him with certain conscious or subconscious reservations and stipulations, He will give us directions accordingly. But if we go all the way with Him, and make the ultimate commitment, He will give us vastly different directions. This means telling Him that we want our lives to affect every nation on earth for the extension of His Kingdom, and that the price tag is up to Him. Simply put, our levels of abandonment to God determine God's levels of directions to us. Yielding our will to His also means following Biblical principles for God's revealed will to be carried out, as you can see from the following story.

An elderly friend, whom Jim and I had known for many years, was dying. On one of the many occasions when we were at his bedside, he asked me to explain a question that had puzzled him for years. The question was why he was not in foreign missionary service after repeated unsuccessful attempts to carry out a vision and call he (and we) believed God had given him in earlier years. I asked, "Were you willing to submit to the authority of others for God to put you in the ministry and fulfill your desires and vision?" His answer was evasive. We had observed an absence of this basic principle operating in his life. Sadly, he died unfulfilled.

Only when we totally surrender our wills to God by making Jesus Christ our Lord and Master does the action really start in the Christian life. And there is not an area of our lives that is more important to surrender to God's will than in relation to having God's directions for a life partner, in God's timing. No decision will more affect our lives or the lives of future generations negatively or positively, outside choosing Jesus Christ as our Lord and Savior. How much heartache, frustration, and unfulfilled expectations come from taking the matter of marriage into our own hands! My mother, in her homespun wisdom, used to say, "Any fool can get married," meaning that it takes wisdom to wait on God and let Him direct us to the right person at the right time—one who will match our temperament, giftings, strengths, weaknesses, and spiritual ministries.

Jim and Joy

I took marriage very seriously. Jim Dawson had been a good friend of mine for some time before he expressed a desire to have a serious friendship in regard to our futures. My response was that if God wanted me to marry him, two things would have to happen. One, God would have to give me a deep-seated, unshakable conviction within my spirit that this was His will for me. Two, God would have to cause me to fall in love with him. Well, as I sought God for direction, He really did a number on me on both counts—big-time!

As I write this book, we have been married for fifty-three years. With 100 percent honesty, we can say that we love each other more deeply and tenderly than ever.

Our son, John, and daughter, Jill, took marriage equally seriously. They not only sought God diligently until they knew they had heard His voice concerning His choice for their life partners, but humbly submitted their impressions to us. Jim, and I in turn, took our responsibility as a spiritual covering over them very seriously and sought God until we knew we had heard His voice equally clearly. Both of our children's impressions were correct, and time has abundantly confirmed that joyous and fulfilling fact. The dedication of this book does not contain a spelling error where I refer to my daughter and son as "in-love" not "in-law."

John and Julie

When John was a young, single missionary in YWAM, he told God he wanted to establish an effective ministry as a priority over concerning himself about looking for a life partner. He determined not to date any girls and informed the Almighty that He would have to drop somebody on him, because he was not looking. In other words, God would have to take the initiative and make the signals starkly clear. Apparently, God welcomed the opportunity.

John was part of a YWAM mobile training team who were ministering at an Assemblies of God church in northern California during one week. At a time of interviewing people as possible candidates for overseas YWAM outreach opportunities,

John found himself in the presence of a very attractive young woman with an "hourglass figure" who was applying to go to Africa.

He heard a distinct voice speaking into his mind, "This is your wife." Assuming this was the perfect setup of how the enemy would want to derail him, he excused himself for a moment, stepped back into the corridor, closed the door of the interview room and firmly whispered, "I rebuke you, Satan and demons, in the name of the Lord Jesus Christ." He returned to continue the interview.

At the end of the week's ministry assignment, a couple from the church gave a farewell party for the team. John and the young woman, Julie, found themselves the last to leave, without any maneuvering on either of their parts. John had no transportation; Julie did, so she offered to drive him back to where he was staying.

John started to realize how many times over the past week he had found himself teamed up in some way with this girl, without either of them being the explanation. Was it just coincidence, or a God-incidence? Could God possibly be up to something? Was John presumptuous in rebuking the devil when that initial impression came out of the blue? And besides, he was definitely attracted to her.

That night he told her what he was thinking and said he would spend the next week asking God if he were to pursue a relationship with her. She said she was experiencing the same thoughts and would appreciate time to seek God's counsel also.

One week later, John called us in Los Angeles, telling us what was going on and saying that he had received what he believed was God's guidance to pursue a relationship with Julie. She also had guidance to go ahead. John asked us to seek God for confirmation, or otherwise, about a girl we had never met. He assured us that he did not want to waste a minute on a friendship that was not in the will of God.

It was several weeks before we were able to contact John again. When we did, I said to him, "You'll need to fasten your seat belt while I tell you how and what God spoke to me." I shared that I had simply asked God, "Is John to pursue Julie in a serious friendship?" God spoke into my mind, "Turn to Second Kings, chapter fourteen." I hadn't a clue what was in that chapter until I looked it up and found verse nine, "Give your daughter to my son for a wife." *Wow!* I could hardly believe my eyes.

Numerous times over the ensuing months when Jim and I kept seeking God for either confirmation or correction, the answers from God were consistently the same: "This is right." Time has proven that we were all undoubtedly hearing God's voice.

David and Katiucia

It is a great joy to be able to share, that by God's grace, the first of a third generation of Dawsons, our grandson, David, has waited on God to hear His voice for the choice of his life partner. Here is his story:

> It was five years since I had a girlfriend. God had made it clear to me that my most important priority was to keep focused on my relationship with Him. That meant I had no

desire to date and play the field, and had resigned myself to wait for God to show me the right girl, at the right time.

I knew that God was preparing someone especially for me and that in His timing I would fall hopelessly in love. I did not know when that would be, but I was looking for a sign as obvious as God's tapping me on the shoulder and pointing her out.

Ever since I surrendered my will to the Lord five years previously, God had kept me on a very short leash regarding girls. Any time I was remotely interested in a nice girl, I would ask the Lord about her. I had always heard that quiet but clear voice of the Holy Spirit saying, "No, that's not the one for you." Although I often had difficulty in discerning God's voice on other matters, I could always hear God distinctly on this subject. I was extremely apprehensive about getting into a relationship of my own making, knowing how messy that can be.

A beautiful Brazilian girl named Katiucia (pronounced Ka-too-shia) and I were on the staff of YWAM School of Ministry Development in Los Angeles. I had every opportunity to observe the godly character of this young woman who had been in YWAM for eighteen months and had learned to speak fluent English. But I had sensed God's warning that it was not the time for me to be thinking about having a romantic relationship with anyone. So that was that.

Three months went by and we found ourselves busily preparing with one other person, to co-lead a team on a nearly three-month-long intensive summer outreach in New York's inner city. In the middle of this hectic time of preparation, God began to do something in my heart. It was strictly initiated by

Him and took me by surprise. The timing defied all human reasoning and it shook me up. (YWAM leaders are wisely cautioned against having romantic relationships on outreaches.)

One day, I was with some YWAM friends in the auditorium where I was working on the sound system. I heard someone come in the door behind me. I turned around and saw my friend Katiucia standing there. In that electrifying moment, God did it. It seemed like He was advertising this young woman and showing her off to me. For the first time I saw her through God's eyes. I was in awe. I had never seen a girl so beautiful in all my life. Her smile captivated me. She seemed to be overflowing with the Holy Spirit. And, in that moment, Katiucia exemplified a purity, strength of character and youthful joy that I had never seen in a girl before.

I recognized that the thoughts I was thinking did not have the quality of my own, but were coming from the voice of God. I had long since recognized the voice of self and satan which always drives for self-gratification. This was totally different. The mixture of peace and excitement that filled my heart about Katiucia could only be from God. I had never experienced anything like this before. God had undeniably tapped me on the shoulder, gotten my attention, and pointed her out to me. Even so, I still pursued God diligently for confirmation, which He faithfully gave me.

Weeks later we found out that we had both felt the same stirrings by the Holy Spirit in our hearts for one another, but both of us had kept them hidden. In God's timing, when we were both certain of God's will for our future lives together, we submitted our directions to both our parents and grandparents. They in turn, had strong confirmation from the

Lord that we were in the center of God's perfect will. We were married in Brazil after the summer outreach, and stayed there for some months while I learned to speak Portuguese before returning to Los Angeles.

Now, dear reader, you may be thinking, *Well, that all sounds wonderful for the Dawson clan, but I didn't have the same opportunities surrounding my life to influence me to make those kinds of choices.* Or you may be realizing that you never waited on God and sought to hear His voice and know His timing about a life partner, even when you could have.

Don't despair. God's plans for your future are bigger than your past failures, provided you acknowledge and repent of past mistakes and want only to live for His glory in His way now. God specializes in making lemonade out of lemons.

I am longing and praying that many young people particularly, and their parents will read this book and be inspired, encouraged and motivated by these shared testimonies to go God's way.

You ask, "Why their parents?" Because so few parents take their responsibility of being the covering they should be for their children before marriage, as has been described. Even if your children don't want you to seek God on their behalf, as parents you have a responsibility before God to do so; and to warn them if necessary, if you believe they are making the wrong choices.

Waiting Before the Lord

Perhaps the most difficult condition to fulfill is the next one: Waiting before the Lord—giving Him protracted time, if necessary, to speak, and listening to His voice with our attention focused on His person. I like to picture Him on His throne in His dazzling beauty, magnificent splendor and supreme authority.

We must ask ourselves this burning question: How much serious listening time do we give God, as a way of life—time, not just for answers to our questions, but for anything He may want to say to us? The apostle Peter was president of the "Let Us" club—always projecting his good ideas. But we notice that God was uniquely unimpressed, especially on the Mount of Transfiguration, when He spoke audibly out of heaven in response to Peter and said, "This is my Son, whom I love. *Listen* to him!" (Mark 9:7 NIV, emphasis added). Hear the heart-cry of God calling His people then and now to do the same thing in Psalm 81:11–13 (emphasis added):

> But My people would not heed My voice,
> And Israel would have none of Me.
> So I gave them over to their own stubborn heart,
> To walk in their own counsels.
> Oh, that My people would *listen* to Me,
> That Israel would walk in My ways!

Peter had to radically change his ways for God's destiny to be fulfilled for his life. So did I, for the same reason. No one needed to learn to wait on God more than this author! But, thank God, He can make our greatest points of weakness our greatest strengths when we keep yielding to the Holy Spirit's disciplines in the fear of the Lord.

It was Saturday, December 19, 1998. For weeks it had

been announced on Christian TV that the Los Angeles International Church, known as the Dream Center, would be giving away many thousands of practical Christmas gifts to the less-fortunate people of the inner city in Los Angeles. Benny Hinn Ministries had donated a large sum of money for this purpose, and Benny was going to be there in person to minister to the people in the early winter's evening, outdoors.

I had a desire to be a part of this evangelistic outreach, so I started to seek God around noon to see if this was also His desire. Jim joined me, but we received no direction, although we kept pressing in to God for hours, literally. Jim was understandably sorely tempted to give up on this guidance project, but I kept saying that I could not understand why the desire to go remained so strong when I had asked God to lift it from me if it was not from Him. So we hung in there without being diverted, although we still had no answer, even when it went past the time that Benny Hinn would be ministering to the inevitable thousands who would not want to miss this unique opportunity to be blessed.

I got ready to leave home immediately, should God's direction come to us to still go. At the same time, I totally relinquished the desire to go into God's hands, and praised and worshiped Him. At 5:20 P.M. God broke through, directing Jim to Judges 18:6, "Go in peace. Your journey has the LORD's approval" (NIV). We were out the door in minutes.

As we neared the Dream Center, with parked cars fully lining the many surrounding streets, I said to Jim, "Drive right up to the front entrance. I'm believing God for miracle parking." Jim cooperated. I jumped out of the car and introduced myself to a man sitting behind the wheel of a van parked right at the entrance. He said he knew me, that he was just leaving, that Benny Hinn had been and gone, and that he would be delighted to give us the parking spot!

Long lines of people were receiving their gifts, others were crowded around the large platform where a Christmas program was in progress, while others were visiting the many booths representing the scores of different evangelistic outreaches of the Dream Center.

Jim and I wandered around the grounds, with our spiritual antennae on full alert, trying to discern why God had kept us waiting more than five hours to tell us to come to this place at this time.

When we came to Jim Bakker's ministry booth, while buying his latest book, a senior staff member recognized me and asked us if we would like to visit with Jim and his new wife of three-and-a-half months, Lori. Sensing God was up to something, we immediately accepted the invitation.

Jim Bakker was working in ministry at the Dream Center with Pastors Tommy and Matthew Barnett, and Lori had been the leader of a ministry to battered and needy women at Tommy Barnett's church in Phoenix, Arizona.

Jim Bakker had been greatly used of God in 1976 to raise money on TV to enable a contingent of seventy university students from Egypt to participate in YWAM's Olympic Games Outreach in Montreal, Canada. Jim heard about the needs when he was interviewing me on one of the several occasions I was a guest on his TV programs. Without Jim's sensitivity and obedience to the promptings of the Holy Spirit at that time, I seriously doubt whether any of those dedicated young people would have been able to participate in that vital time of training and witnessing to the Arabic-speaking athletes and visitors at the Olympics. I have been forever grateful to God and Jim Bakker.

After greeting us warmly, Jim and Lori shared the remarkable story of how God brought them together. We were thrilled to hear how God's redemptive purposes were being worked out in two previously shattered lives. As they shared, their brokenness before the Lord and genuine God-given burden to reach out to hurting, lost people was obvious.

Early in our visit, Jim Bakker casually mentioned that he was to conduct a wedding that evening. After about an hour of listening with rapt attention to the radical reality of God's workings in and through Jim and Lori, I asked Jim when he was going to the wedding. Glancing at his watch he said, "Oh, I think right about now would be fine." We told them that we would leave straight away and thanked them profusely for giving us the pleasure of being with them.

Jim said, "Why leave now? We're having it right here. We'd be privileged for you to join in with us."

I said, "Where are the bride and groom?"

He said, "Right there," pointing to a couple in jeans, sweaters and sneakers, who had been quietly sitting in the room, whom I had never met!

Jim explained that they were on staff at the Dream Center, and had planned for the wedding ceremony to be performed in a few days' time. But they discovered that afternoon that Jim Bakker had an unexpected scheduling conflict, and the only time he could perform the wedding was that evening.

As this was obviously no problem to all concerned, we decided to stay and go with the flow. By now I had decided that this was the surprise-a-minute night of all time and was totally intrigued. Vernon and Mary McClellan, who had worked with Jim Bakker, heading up his worldwide missions program and serving as guest hosts at Heritage Village years before, had arrived in the Bakkers' little room just ahead of us and were equally going with the flow. Both of them are now on the Benny Hinn crusade team. As Vernon ministers as an anointed and accomplished violinist, we managed to persuade him to get his violin out of the trunk of his car and give us a suitable violin solo. What could be better?

At this point, Lori grabbed some red silk roses out of a vase, wrapped them in some Christmas ribbons and placed them in the bride's hands. That made the bouquet. Everything was falling into place beautifully with an absence of ostentation or sweat, but, a lot of relaxed joy. All evening, Jim Bakker was dressed in jeans, a casual blue shirt and denim jacket, complete with a baseball cap. The whole setup communicated without words, "Why change anything?" He didn't.

Jim conducted the wedding ceremony with quiet reverence and dignity. While the surroundings were casual with a capital C, there was no sense of flippancy. We were deeply touched by the solemnity of the occasion devoid of the usual trappings, and the obvious sweet presence of the Lord. I whispered to Mary, "Isn't this fabulous?" as Vernon softly played a medley of appropriate and beautiful hymns on his violin. When Jim asked Lori to share something from her heart with the bride and groom, she talked about how impressed she had been when in Australia recently the leader of the Aglow International in Australia, Mrs. Joan Morton, had said the secret of her many years of successful marriage was that she and her husband were true servants to one another.

After the vows were exchanged, I nearly swallowed my tonsils when Jim Bakker quietly said, "Now our dear sister Joy will bring the Word of the Lord to us." In God's mercy, the officiating minister decided to have a prayer first, which gave me a few minutes to whisper to my husband, Jim, "If ever I needed you to intercede for me, it's now," and then cast myself on God to *listen to His voice.*

As always, He came through just in time. He directed me to share some of the secrets of our fifty years of a very successful marriage.

One of those secrets is that we have always recognized, released, and supported each other to minister according to our individual ministry giftings. This way we complete each other and never compete with each other. Another is the way we seek God together as a way of life until we hear His voice to know His will over matters large and small, and intercede frequently together for many others. And it's always been important for us to be each other's closest friend and confidant.

God then gave me a powerful blessing prayer for the newlyweds.

We left our little group that night totally fulfilled, knowing God's purposes had been accomplished through seeing the wisdom of waiting on God for His answers to our inquiries. Had we left our home any sooner, we would have missed one of the most unusual, interesting, intriguing, and enjoyable evenings of our lives.

At the time of this book going to print, Jim and Lori Bakker are developing a camp in Florida for needy innercity children called Camp Hope.

Recognizing the Source of the Voice

The Sixth Condition to fulfill to be sure we hear God's voice is to recognize that there are three sources from which impressions can come to us. We have already established the validity of the first voice, the voice of God. The second is the voice of self, which comes from either our human reasoning or from our own desires. Our human reasoning is what we think the answer should be. The Bible does not leave us in any doubt about the folly of relying on that source, as we can see from the following Scriptures.

- "He who trusts in his own mind is a fool" (Proverbs 28:26 RSV).

- "Trust in the LORD with all your heart, and lean not on your own understanding [or insight]; in all your ways acknowledge Him, and He shall direct your paths" (Proverbs 3:5–6).

- "Casting down arguments . . . bringing every thought into captivity to the obedience of Christ" (2 Corinthians 10:5). The study notes in the margin of my King James version say that the word *arguments* can also mean "reasonings."

- "'For My thoughts are not your thoughts, nor are your ways My ways,' says the LORD" (Isaiah 55:8).

Impressions can also come from our desires, which are often strong, so we need to come to the place where we honestly say to God as Jesus did, "Not My will, but Yours, be done" (Luke 22:42). By an act of our wills, we die to what we think and what we want, and believe God accepts the death to our self life that we offer Him.

As we will it to be so and trust Him, He makes it so. And dead people don't talk. Romans 6:11 describes the process: "Likewise you also, reckon yourselves to be dead indeed to sin [or self], but alive to God in Christ Jesus our Lord." When you have truly done this, you know you are in neutral gear.

Our daughter, Jill, shares the next story of a valuable lesson we learned as a family, when seeking God together for His directions.

I was about eleven years old and for a number of years had been attending Christian children's camps during two of our school vacation periods. The camp, called Children's Bible Crusade, focused more on spiritual values. Another camp I attended only once focused more on games and entertainment.

On one occasion, when it came time for us to know if I was to go to camp, I expressed my desire to have a change from the Children's Bible Crusade and go to another camp. As a way of life, we sought for God's directions in prayer as a family. This was no exception. After doing so, both my parents and I believed we had impressions that I was to attend the one for which I had expressed a desire. My brother John, who was 15 years old, said he believed the impression he had received was that I was not to attend this camp.

Because of the "majority rule" factor, we pursued the enrollment at my favored camp, only to find they were completely booked. After repeated inquiries in case of possible cancellations, with only two days before the camps started, John reminded us of the negative direction he had received concerning my going to this camp.

Dad, Mom, and I humbled ourselves before God, confessing that we had too easily disregarded John's impression, and we all sought God again. This time we all heard God speaking into our spirits, accompanied by His peace, that I was to go to the Children's Bible Crusade camp. The question now was, at this eleventh hour, would they take me? A phone call later, the answer was, "Yes." At that camp, I experienced God's blessing and drew closer to Him.

My mom explained to us that we had learned a valuable lesson as a family, never to make a decision until we were all in unity, and that we should have gone back to the Lord (after the first time we sought Him) to show us why we had differing impressions. God would have brought us to unity by revealing to us that all except John had not sufficiently died to our human reasonings and/or desires.

We must also recognize that satanic and demonic powers can bring impressions to our minds. They can quote and misquote Scriptures and even direct us to specific Scriptures. The voices of demonic spirits are often loud, urgent, and insistent, as Satan is always trying to precipitate a crisis, and trying to get us to act hastily. Whereas, the voice of the Lord is quiet but persistent, motivating us to come aside and quietly wait and listen. The Word of God tells us in James 4:7, "Submit to God. Resist the devil and he will flee from you." We can always test the source of our impressions.

I have heard the voice of the enemy. One day I was having an effective time in intercession alone with God when three times I received loud impressions in my spirit, interrupting my prayers, telling me to go quickly to a new convert I was discipling because she was in urgent need of my help. She lived on the other side of the city and quite a long distance from my home. I had already planned to go and visit her that evening.

I had already experienced that one of the enemy's tactics is to try to bring diversions and distractions to us whenever we take seriously the ministry of intercession. So I checked the source of this urgent redirection of my time and energy. I asked the Lord to confirm these impressions if they were from Him and waited. Nothing. I took authority over the powers of darkness in the name of the Lord Jesus Christ, silencing them on the basis of God's Word, quoting James 4:7: "Therefore submit to God. Resist the devil and he will flee from you."

I went on praying, and there were no more distracting voices, just a wonderful peace that I was in the center of God's will. Later, I thought about Satan's tactics and character in relation to this incident. They interrupted the call of God to intercede for others, trying to get me to stop; and the voice was loud, insistent, and demanding. Our Shepherd, Jesus, leads. Satanic voices goad and prod.

Later that evening, when I went to the new convert's home, she said that she had just accepted a job, taking her three young children with her that day. If I had followed the voice of the enemy, I would have found no one at home and been in total confusion and frustration. When God gives us a mission, follow through on it and do not be distracted by other people's demands or subtle satanic suggestions. They can come disguised in many different forms, trying to keep us from making God's priorities our priorities. The choice is ours.

The most powerful way to silence the voice of the enemy is to quote the Word of God in faith to him as Jesus did when He was on earth (see Luke 4:1–12). Other appropriate Scriptures are, "And they overcame him by the blood of the Lamb and by the word of their testimony" (Revelation 12:11); and "For this purpose the Son of God was manifested, that He might destroy the works of the devil" (1 John 3:8).

Command all demonic forces to be silent in the all-powerful name of the Lord Jesus Christ, exercising faith in that name which is above every other name. Now, with the voice of self and Satan silenced, there's only God's voice left to speak. Just in case you are not convinced that demonic voices can give impressions to the most sincere Christians, I will illustrate.

One Saturday night when we lived in New Zealand, I was taking my turn ministering downtown in the Teen Challenge work in which we were heavily involved. Jim and I took turns staying home with the children. That night it was Jim's turn. Upon my returning home late, Jim shared with me that he had been earnestly seeking God for some encouraging Scriptures to give to our dear pastor friend who was soon leaving on a potentially dangerous mission to Russia to encourage "underground" Christians at a time when there was much persecution from the Communist government.

Jim was obviously shocked and shaken because of the clear impressions that came into his mind, which were "Jeremiah chapter twenty-two, verses eleven and twelve." When he looked them up he read, "For thus says the LORD concerning Shallum . . . king of Judah, . . . who went from this place: 'He shall not return here anymore, but he shall die in the place where they have led him captive, and shall see this land no more.'"

I immediately responded by asking Jim if he had silenced the voices of demonic spirits before seeking God. He thought back and then said, "No, I forgot" although it had long been a way of life with Jim to deal with the enemy first. We then took authority over the enemy and sought God again. Immediately God directed us to wonderfully assuring Scriptures of protection for our precious pastor. We later shared them with him, and they became a source of significant comfort and assurance to him as he encountered an ugly situation from which God miraculously delivered him through an angelic visitation.

Always thank God that He will answer you in His way and in His timing. This will avoid frustration, confusion, unbelief, and possible resentment and rebellion toward God if He does not answer within your presumed time frame.

The following verses, memorized, become a great source of comfort and assurance, especially during a prolonged waiting time.

- "But as for me, my prayer is to You, O Lord, in the acceptable time; O God, in the multitude of Your mercy, hear me in the truth of Your salvation" (Psalm 69:13). The Revised Standard Version renders the last clause of this verse as follows: "in the abundance of thy steadfast love answer me."

- "Therefore I will look to the Lord; I will wait for the God of my salvation. My God will hear me" (Micah 7:7).

- "I wait for You O Lord; / You will answer O Lord, my God" (Micah 7:7 RSV)

Throughout this chapter, I have repeatedly referred to the need to wait quietly in God's presence. Perhaps you would identify with a sincere person who wrote me a letter saying, "My problem is that, while I am waiting on God, my mind wanders. I find that I spend most of my time steering my attention back to waiting. Can you help me?"

My reply was: "I suggest that your mind will not wander on to other subjects when listening to hear God's voice when you understand *who He is* you're seeking."

Can you imagine being in the Oval Office at the White House for a conversation with the President of the United States and asking him a question—and then letting your mind wander on to unrelated things? You are in charge of your mind. It does not wander without your control. Not concentrating on the President's reply would be unthinkable! How much more when you are listening for direction from the Creator and Sustainer of the universe. Also, if you are listening with childlike faith, you will be expecting an answer, and you will not want to miss it by choosing to think of other things. God rewards diligent seekers (see Hebrews 11:6). How desperate are you to know God has spoken to you? How desperate are you for God, period?

Are you content with constantly having secondhand revelation of truth, and only hearing from God through others? Or will you pay any price to hear God as a way of life for yourself? When the Israelites were standing in the distance from Mount Sinai and God showed up with a display of His awesome power, they witnessed the thunderings, lightning flashes, the blast of the trumpet, the mountain smoking and quaking and said to Moses, "You speak with us, and we will hear; but let not God speak with us, lest we die" (Exodus 20:19). On the other hand, Moses was desperate for personal, intimate friendship with God, and his reaction was to draw near the thick darkness "where God was," to hear His voice (see Exodus 19:21).

I would rather pay the price to hear God's voice personally, regardless of how difficult the circumstances may be, than to have to settle for always hearing from Him secondhand. How about you?

Section

3

Twenty-Four Ways God Speaks

$\mathscr{P}$robably one of the most fascinating aspects of hearing God's voice is discovering the great variety of ways in which He has chosen to communicate with us. In this section I'm going to share twenty-four ways with you.

There are no dull moments on this adventurous journey of walking and talking with our fabulous friend, God. That is, of course, if we refuse to limit Him. God wants to bring us to the place where our deepest level of excitement and fulfillment comes not from what He says or in the way He chooses to say it, but because of who He is—the Lover of our souls. I repeatedly stand in awe and wonder when He speaks to me. Hearing His voice never becomes commonplace, although it has long been a way of life for me.

God Speaks Through His Word

God often quickens Scriptures to us by the Holy Spirit in our daily devotional reading of the Bible. We may be needing counsel for a problem we're facing or for direction. "Your statutes are my delight; they are my counselors," said David in Psalm 119:24 (NIV). He also prayed, "Direct my steps by Your word, and let no iniquity have dominion over me" (Psalm 119:133 NKJV).

To whom do you go first when you have a problem? A

family member? A friend via the telephone? A pastoral staff member from your church? A psychiatrist? Why not go to the source of infinite knowledge and wisdom, the ultimate counselor as described in Isaiah 9:6? He not only has all the answers, He does not charge us anything and everything is kept in the closest confidence. You can't beat that.

At one time, when we lived in New Zealand, we had an evangelist who had a hole in his heart staying with us. His strength was severely limited and his physical condition was critical, to say the least. The doctors had said that he was inoperable. (There have been tremendous advances in medical science since those days.) However, God gave Jim and me the faith to believe for a miracle healing for our friend, and we prayed that God would speak to him directly before we shared our convictions with him. One morning, the evangelist told me that God had unquestionably spoken to him in his daily Bible reading and promised him divine healing. He had read, "I have seen his ways, and will heal him; . . . and I will heal him" (Isaiah 57:18–19).

I was encouraged and fascinated, and asked our friend what method of Bible-reading he was using. He simply stated that, as a way of life, he asked God to speak into his mind and to name which book in the Bible he was to read. God's last spoken direction to him was the book of Isaiah. I had never heard of this method and was intrigued. It sure made sense to me, so I immediately applied it to my life with exhilarating and significant results. Looking back, I now understand that this is how I learned to hear God's voice on a regular basis, and my daily reading of God's Word became an exciting adventure. I repeatedly noticed that answers to personal issues and problems related to those of others I had to counsel were often right there in my daily reading of the Scriptures.

Now, back to the evangelist friend's need. One evening, when a few of our closest friends were praying fervently in their separate homes, and I was praying alone, God directed Jim to lay his hands on our desperately needy friend's heart and pray the prayer of faith for his complete recovery. As a result, Jim actually felt the heart beneath his hands jerking as Doctor God performed His surgery and closed the hole. The evangelist was totally healed and was greatly used of God for many years. What a mighty, awesome God we serve. We delight to give Him all the glory.

God frequently speaks to me from His Word. I totally relate to David's prayer, "Direct me in the path of Your commands, for there I find delight" (Psalm 119:35 NIV). In fact, I believe the answers for anything I'll ever need to know are in God's Word, should He choose that method to speak to me. I have proved it more times than I can remember or count.

This should not be too surprising as the Bible is the living Word of the living God, and as such, we should be expecting Him to speak from it. John 1:14 describes the Lord Jesus, "The Word became flesh and dwelt among us, and we beheld His glory . . ." It saddens me when the most well-meaning, sincere and often wonderful Christians put limitations on the ways God should or should not speak to us from His Word.

The Bible is the inspired Word of God, which I like to think of as His love letter to us; and is given to us for the purpose of understanding His character and ways. And because it is God-breathed (see 2 Timothy 3:16), it is pulsating with life—His life, which is limitless and eternal.

We know that God has gone to incredible lengths to preserve all of His Word so that we can not only know Him from its pages today, but hear His voice speaking personally and intimately to us. I want to make it crystal clear that we should never just open the Bible randomly, and casually put our finger on a verse, and automatically go and do whatever it says. What if we did that and read that Judas hanged himself (see Matthew 27:5), then repeated the action, and landed upon the verse which says "Go and do likewise" (Luke 10:37)?

- On the other hand, when we approach God in the fear of the Lord, *He can sovereignly open the Bible to us at a time of need and direct our eyes to the exact verse or verses that will give us His answers.* This method always includes a strong conviction or inner witness from the Holy Spirit accompanied by God's supernatural peace that He has spoken. I have heard and read about numbers of internationally known, respected spiritual leaders who have experienced this simple method in God's communication system with remarkable results.

In Psalm 119:105, God tells us that His Word will give us direction for the next thing we have to do, as well as give us understanding of what we are to be doing in the future. Isn't that reassuring? It reads: "Your word is a lamp to my feet [the immediate need] and a light to my path" [what's ahead]. The next two stories illustrate this promise.

I had just finished a phone call during which I had been invited to speak at an overflow conference that was being planned because the originally advertised conference was completely booked. I was one of the speakers and the need to have the same speakers for the overflow crowd was obvious. The ministry opportunities for me were far better than in the originally planned conference, and I had no scheduling conflict. I could do both. I said I would seek the Lord and get back to them with whatever the Lord showed me. I fully expected Him to say "Yes."

Jim and I waited on God together, dying to all human reasoning and desire, and listened for God's answer, quoting James 4:7 to the powers of darkness first so that they could not speak in case they were around. They are not omnipresent.

I felt impressed to open my Bible. Immediately my eyes were directed to Numbers 14:44: "But they presumed to go up . . ." and then Numbers 15:30–31: "But the person who does anything presumptuously, whether he is native-born or a stranger, that one brings reproach on the LORD, and he shall be cut off from among his people. Because he has despised the word of the LORD, and has broken His commandment, that person shall be completely cut off; his guilt shall be upon him."

I was surprised, but instantly knew that those verses were a solemn warning from the Lord not to presume anything. The longer we sought the Lord, the more He repeatedly spoke into my spirit that I was not to accept this additional invitation. This was accompanied by a strong conviction and peace in both Jim and me that His will had been revealed.

I thanked God from a deeply grateful heart that He had kept me from the sin of presumption by speaking to me through His Word. Circumstances later proved that this decision was 100 percent correct.

Here's a fascinating story with the same method of divine

guidance that a woman named Dawn experienced after hearing me give a series of messages on this subject at her church in San Diego. Dawn said that God had been speaking to her about buying a plane ticket for her friend who was going to a prayer conference. She obeyed. Then she realized that her friend needed money for the conference registration fee. Neither Dawn nor her friend had the money.

Soon after that, God strongly impressed upon Dawn's spirit, like a mental picture, her pastor and his wife, Joe and Tricia Rhodes, with the understanding that they were to pay the conference registration fee. Dawn told the Lord that she needed some undeniable confirmation from the Scriptures that He had spoken to her, before approaching the Rhodes by phone.

In obedience to what she had been taught, she took authority over any demonic spirits that may have been around and rebuked them in Jesus' name. Then she felt led to open her Bible, and immediately her eyes fell on the words, "The men of Rhodes traded with you," from Ezekiel 27:15 (NIV).

Dawn said that she knew this was God's amazing way of confirming His voice to her, because she would have been nervous about asking her pastors to give her friend the money without this kind of incredible certainty.

Dawn said she never knew the name Rhodes was in the Bible (Join the club!). She has since found out that many versions of the Bible do not use the name Rhodes, but the NIV does, and that is the Bible she was using.

What an ingenious God! Nobody knows what is in the Bible like the author of the Book—God Himself—and He knows every word of every version. Needless to say, Pastors Joe and Tricia Rhodes were intrigued to know their names were in the Bible and delighted that God had spoken in such a direct way; and they joyfully cooperated to meet the need.

The following list includes more ways God speaks through His Word.

- When it is in literature.

- When being quoted through the ministries of preaching and teaching, shared testimonies, or music.

- When specific portions are given by a person of proven character and ministry who has been directed by the Holy Spirit to do so to an individual or group.

- When we receive revelation by the Holy Spirit through meditation. Meditating on the Scriptures is simply inviting the Holy Spirit to shine the light of God's truth upon your mind as you slowly, repeatedly read word-by-word, line-by-line, believing for supernatural insights into the hidden truths below the surface meaning. Because the Bible is the living Word of the living God, we find we can receive fresh revelation of truth on any portions of it that we've read many times before, as we continue to meditate as described.

  One ounce of meditation is worth a ton of memorization, because meditation produces revelation, and revelation is the greatest incentive to motivate worship and obedience. You will find an additional resource on this subject in Appendix C.

- When it is on billboards. We must never underestimate the convicting power of the Word of God. I was driving along a highway one day when I glanced at the billboard outside the Methodist church that I frequently passed. This church regularly changed Scripture verses on their billboard and I always looked to see what they displayed. When I read the verse, I was immediately convicted of a sin and repented before the Lord. I have long since forgotten the Scripture and the sin, but never forgotten the experience. Subsequently I've prayed many times that God's people would catch the vision of putting the Word of God on billboards in conspicuous places.

- God speaks through His Word even when an individual reads it sporadically but with a sincere desire to know God personally. For example, I had a close friend who had everything that, to all appearances, would bring fulfillment to her life. She was happily married to a successful businessman; had two lovely daughters; lived in a beautiful home in a choice location; enjoyed excellent health; and had an outgoing personality and plenty of friends, but she still felt empty and unfulfilled.

  One day when standing on the balcony of her home she looked up at the sky and said to herself, "There is a God up there, but I don't know Him."

  At times when she felt inclined, she would read her Bible. This caused her to want to know God personally. She was arrested by a verse of Scripture, "Seek, and you will find" (Luke 11:9).

  One afternoon she knelt beside her bed and prayed for God to show her the way.

  A few nights later, He answered by giving her three consecutive dreams. In the first one she saw the evil face of the devil and heard him say, "I will offer you all the things of the world." Then she saw the Lord Jesus on the cross, blood flowing from His wounds: and He simply said "I will give you eternal life." Then a voice boomed out, "You choose." Her response was, to turn to the Lord, repent of her sins, and ask for His forgiveness and say, "I choose You, Jesus Christ, as my Lord."

When she woke up, she realized the enormous implications of the dreams and reiterated her choice. She realized that her choice had determined her destiny. She remained true to her life's commitment to follow Christ and was mightily used of God to bring others to Him in the power of the Holy Spirit.

- God also speaks from His Word when it has been memorized, and then quickened by the Holy Spirit to meet a need. I am reminded of an illustration from my life of how a memorized Scripture was powerfully used of God to encourage me in a time of great transition.

  The year was 1971. I had returned home to New Zealand from three-and-a-half months of Bible teaching in about five nations with my dear husband's total approval. Jim and I had been stirred in our spirits about his leaving secular employment, relinquishing all our financial securities, house, car, family, and friends and joining YWAM as unsalaried missionaries and going to the United States—all of this with two teenagers!

  We knew of no ongoing financial support for us whatsoever. We simply knew the character of God and the promises from His Word. It was absolutely crucial that we receive strong, clear directions from the Lord if this in fact was His will for us as a family.

The stirrings from the Holy Spirit continued unabated. At this time, for three whole weeks I kept hearing in my spirit a verse of Scripture I had memorized. It was, "It is God Who works in you both to will and to do for His good pleasure" (Philippians 2:13). At first I wondered why these impressions persisted, until I came to the understanding that it was God's way of saying to us that it was God who was stirring us, putting these thoughts and desires into our hearts, preparing us to take the big step of obedience and faith to become lifetime missionaries to the nations.

Another way that God explained why He kept speaking Philippians 2:13 to me happened in this way. One evening when we were having our daily family worship time after the evening meal, Jim was directed by the Lord to read through Luke chapter 5. When he came to the words, "'Do not be afraid. From now on you will catch men.' So when they had brought their boats to land, they forsook all and followed Him" (vv. 10–11), we had the strongest witness in our spirits that God had given us His mandate from His Word. Another Scripture that stood out, or seemed to light up every time we read it, was, "In Thee they trusted, and were not disappointed" (Psalm 22:5 RSV).

• Sometimes the Holy Spirit speaks a Scripture reference (the book, chapter, and at times, the verse) to our minds which specifically addresses a given situation. This is illustrated in the following story from John Bills, my son-in-law and southwest director of YWAM in the United States.

My wife, Jill, and I had just completed directing a discipleship training school in Los Angeles, California, followed by a two-month evangelistic and mercy ministry outreach in various cities and towns in southern Mexico with our staff and students. There were two possible routes back to Los Angeles. One was more direct and the other lengthy, scenic, and more expensive.

I gathered my staff together to seek the Lord for which route we were to take. After resisting the enemy in Jesus' name and dying to our human reasonings and desires, everyone received the same impression in our spirits, *Take the long route home.* This route required us to travel to the Mexican west coast, take a vehicular ferry across to the Baja Peninsula and then go up to California.

Because we were all tired and a few team members were ill, I felt I needed confirmation from God to know that we had heard Him correctly. The Holy Spirit spoke to me to turn to Isaiah 51:10, which says, "Are You not the One who dried up the sea, the waters of the great deep; that made *the depths of the sea a road for the redeemed to cross over?*" Verse eleven says, "*So the ransomed of the* LORD *shall return,* and come to Zion with singing, with everlasting joy on their heads. They shall obtain joy and gladness; sorrow and sighing shall flee away" (emphasis added).

This clear confirmation from God's Word would play a big part in what lay ahead of us. We found a beautiful campground on the west coast of Mexico where the students were able to swim and rest after an exhausting time of ministry to others.

But that night a heavy storm came, and by morning our tents were blown down, and our clothing and food all wet. We were not exactly happy campers! To our surprise, we found the campground full of American tourists, each of whom came to our rescue, repairing our tents, drying our clothes, and inviting each student into their recreational vehicles for a hot meal.

As a result, many of those hospitable Americans gave their lives to Christ as the students shared the purpose of their outreach in Mexico. What looked like anything but a fulfillment of the Word of the Lord to us turned out to be a fruitful witnessing situation and a great blessing.

Before starting out on the return journey, I had gone to the vehicular ferry company to make bookings for our three vehicles to coincide with the date on which God had directed us to leave. I was told there were no spaces available, and that we would have to wait four or five more days for another ferry. Although it was not their regular custom, the agent reluctantly agreed to put our three vehicles with our names on a waiting list.

At dawn, we were the first ones to arrive at the ferry company, right on God's directed timetable for us. I had great confidence that God would come through. After all the other vehicles had been loaded on the ferry, to our delight Jill and I saw our bus full of students drive on, and then our van with our staff. So far, so great! When the agent came to me and said my name was not listed and therefore we couldn't go aboard, we could hardly believe it.

We reflected on the guidance God had given the staff and us, including the Scripture God had so clearly spoken to me. Jill and I chose to believe God would make a way when there appeared to be no way in this testing of our faith.

I felt impressed to get out of our little truck and ask the agent to let me personally see his list as he held it in his hand. I then asked him to remove his thumb from the bottom of the page, and when he did, there was my name. After apologizing, the agent told us to drive on to the only space left on the boat. It was so narrow Jill and I had to literally climb out of the windows; there was no space to open the doors! But we were all on board, with total fulfillment of what our wonderfully faithful friend, God, had spoken to us and had confirmed through His Word.

Isn't God amazing?

After I had given a message one time in a church in northern California on the different ways God speaks, I invited the people to ask God any questions for which they needed answers. I explained that they needed to first fulfill the conditions for hearing God's voice as given to them in the previous evening's teaching, which are also in this book.

During the sharing time, this story emerged. A sixteen-year-old girl said that her mother was always telling her that she (the daughter) was using far too much eye makeup. The daughter was equally convinced that she was not, which produced daily conflict. The girl recalled that I had said that the answer is in the Word of God for anything we will ever need to know, should God choose to use that method to speak to us.

She said, "Okay God, I'll give this teaching a try. Am I

using too much eye makeup?" Immediately an impression came into her spirit, "Turn to Jeremiah chapter four, verse thirty."

She did not have a clue what was in that verse any more than you do, or I did. To her amazement she read, "Though you enlarge your eyes with paint, in vain you will make yourself fair; your lovers will despise you; they will seek your life." That did it. During the sharing time that followed, she said she was going home to tell her mom that she was right.

A woman who had been listening to my teaching tapes wrote me a letter describing what happened when she used this same method. She had lost her keys, and after searching everywhere and recruiting others in her home to help her, was frustrated, and her agenda ground to a halt. She then remembered what she had heard on the tapes and said to herself, *Well, I guess Joy Dawson would have asked God to tell her where the keys were, given this situation, and she'd have a story of how God spoke to her.*

So she said, "Dear God, where are my keys?" and quietly listened instead of fussing and worrying. God answered by speaking into her spirit, "Turn to Leviticus chapter fourteen, and verse forty-seven in your Bible." She read, "And he who lies down in the house shall wash his clothes, and he who eats in the house shall wash his clothes." You're probably thinking, *Well, what on earth has that to do with finding the lost keys?* Everything.

She had washed her clothes, folded them, and put them on the dining room table. When she went to eat her meal, she removed them and put them on her bed. So she followed God's clues from His spoken, living, relevant Word, lifted up the clothes on the bed, and there were the keys. Hallelujah. What a God!

God Speaks Through What We See

Visions

God can speak to us through visions when our eyes are open or when they are closed. He can also give us a mental picture as a means of communicating something to us.

There were major implications in the life of the early church when God spoke in visions to the apostle Peter the Jew, and Cornelius the Gentile centurion in Acts chapter 10. We read, "About the ninth hour of the day he saw clearly in a vision an angel of God coming in and saying to him, 'Cornelius!'" (Acts 10:3). Instructions followed. The same chapter tells us that God appeared to Peter three times in a similar vision with a specific message related to Cornelius. As a result of these two men's steps of obedience to God, the gospel was preached to the Gentiles as well as to the Jews. What an historic breakthrough for the spread of the gospel!

At times, a vision might come in the form of a written script. After I had finished teaching on divine guidance at a large church in northern California, I asked the audience to follow through on the conditions needed to hear God's voice. Then I invited them to ask God whatever they needed Him to say to them, and listen in silent expectation. They did—with remarkable results.

The choir director in that church, Mrs. Bonnie Argue, asked the Lord what special presentation He wanted the choir to prepare for the upcoming Easter services.

God answered by showing her a mental picture of a written script as her eyes were closed with the words, "many infallible proofs." As she continued to seek God, He spoke inaudibly into her spirit saying, "I don't want you to put on the usual Easter cantata. I'm going to give you scene after scene of how I want the choir to act out the events between the resurrection of the Lord Jesus and His ascension, describing 'many infallible proofs.' There will be little emphasis on music."

The next scenario in this multifaceted communication was that my dear friend Bonnie had a series of visions as God showed her in vivid detail what was to be enacted in scene after scene, running parallel with the truths in the Word of God. Then God said, "I will give you the songs. They will include songs related to the Ascension and to the Resurrection." The next thing she needed was the written script for all the actors in the choir.

Bonnie simply inquired of the Lord with a pad and pen in hand, and wrote down what God gave her inspirationally. It flowed easily. God is not short of inspiration and He is the greatest communicator of truth.

I went back to that church at Easter time and heard and saw the whole marvelous, wonderful God-thing! After that experience, Bonnie did not want to go back to the old way of choosing things for the choir to do and asking God to bless them.

Her next question was, "Lord, what do You want the choir to do for Christmas?" God was delighted by this inquiry and poured out His Spirit in revelation on her again, giving her the subject first, "I want the choir to portray Me as the Deliverer."

Then He gave to Bonnie the name of another woman in the church, Marilyn, who had artistic talent and with whom Bonnie was to be linked to bring forth God's purposes in this Spirit-led production. God gave both of them revelation knowledge of how every scene was to be enacted with the accompanying written script. The Holy Spirit gave Marilyn a detailed vision of exactly how to portray angels in dress, color, and movement.

Well ahead of time, God showed these women that they were to book the largest auditorium in the city for three presentations of the drama. They obeyed. At the first performance, the place was totally packed. At the second performance, more than a thousand people were turned away as word got around about the strong spiritual impact that had been made at the first showing.

In spiritual preparation, Bonnie had the choir members fast and pray all through one Saturday at the church for the maximum outpouring of the Spirit to come upon unconverted people as the choir portrayed Jesus as the Deliverer through drama and song in different kinds of lives and circumstances.

Many people came to these performances who never normally attended church, among whom were doctors and scientists, who were so overwrought by the manifest presence of Christ they were openly weeping.

How God yearns to reveal His mind with His creative ideas to those who will have the humility and faith to ask Him, wait upon Him, believe that He will speak, and implicitly obey His orders. It does not matter how mightily God has used the ways we have done it in the past (whatever service to God that represents), we will never know what better way He has to extend His Kingdom until we lay aside our good ideas and agendas, and ask Him to show us if He wants to do a new thing. We are so much more bound by tradition than we have the slightest knowledge. It's sickening and sad. God is never in a mold. Let's do things the Jesus way. His agenda for service came from always listening to the Father for His orders.

Dreams

One night on Christian television I heard the remarkable testimony of a man who had been a leading pornographic moviemaker in the United States. For three nights in regular succession, God had caused him to have vivid dreams about the horrendous judgments from God that are coming on those who reject the Lord Jesus as Savior and Master, as described in the Book of Revelation.

These traumatic experiences shook him so profoundly that he said the only way he could get peace of mind was to surrender his life to Christ and repent of his sins. He did, and became a transformed man.

The following Scripture passage describes this experience.

> For God may speak in one way, or in another,
> Yet man does not perceive it.
> In a dream, in a vision of the night,
> When deep sleep falls upon men,
> While slumbering on their beds,
> Then He opens the ears of men,
> And seals their instruction.
> In order to turn man from his deed,
> And conceal pride from man,
> He keeps back his soul from the Pit,
> And his life from perishing by the sword. (Job 33:14–18)

Angels

Some angels are obvious, some are "unobvious." When Elijah ran away in fear from Jezebel's threat on his life, God sent an angel who baked a cake for him when he was out in

Nowheresville, depressed and depleted. The message through the angel was "Arise and eat," with a refreshing drink included. That meal was so nutritious it lasted him for forty days and nights of traveling. I call that first-class service, and the cook-come-waiter was an obvious heavenly messenger.

There are other times when God speaks through unobvious angels. When the angels came to Lot when he was sitting in the gate of the city of Sodom to warn him and his family to leave that wicked city before God's judgment fell, the angels looked like men and shared a meal with Lot in his house. But they had the authority and power from God to destroy the cities of Sodom and Gomorrah (see Genesis 19:12–24).

In my book *Intercession, Thrilling and Fulfilling,* I share the remarkable story of how God sent an angel to David and Nancy Ravenhill at midnight, warning them of a fire that was threatening to envelop their southern California home. The angel spoke, looked, and acted like a human being, but suddenly disappeared when his mission of helping them with their young children was completed.

Remember my story about our pastor friend who was sent by God on a dangerous mission to Russia when it was under Communist domination? I will elaborate on that story to further illustrate how God communicates through angels.

There are times, when it is in the best interests of the Christian who needs an angelic visitation, that an angel looks like any of the other people in that situation.

Our pastor friend from New Zealand had been given an address of some Christians in Russia with whom he was to meet secretly to encourage them and give them Bibles in their language. He did not know when he left his hotel and arrived at the street address given him that it was the wrong address. After he had knocked on the door of the house, he realized that he was not among believers, but that he was unwelcome and was treated with great suspicion. He was soon surrounded by a mob of hostile Communists. He could not speak their language or understand what they were planning to do with him. Their menacing manner made the atmosphere very tense.

Suddenly, it seemed out of nowhere, a kindly spoken man who looked like everyone else, grabbed the pastor's arm and pulled him away from the angry mob and told him in English to follow him. The pastor told the man the name of the hotel where he was staying. The stranger directed the pastor to get on a certain bus, then boarded it with him and spoke to the bus driver. On the journey the friendly man said very little, but kept smiling reassuringly at our friend. Just as the bus came near the hotel where our friend was staying, the man said, "This is your stop," and then suddenly disappeared.

Our friend pondered the serenity of the man and the quiet authority by which he operated. The more the pastor sought God for understanding about that stranger who saved his life that day and disappeared as quickly as he came, the more he became convinced that God had sent an angel to rescue him. I am equally convinced.

This story has personal significance to me as I had been strongly impressed by the Holy Spirit (just before our pastor left to go on this dangerous mission) to give him an article from *The Alliance Witness* magazine. It was entitled, "I Too Saw an Angel," and was written by Dr. Raymond Edmond, who was president of Wheaton College when Dr. Billy Graham was a student there.

Raymond Edmond and his wife had been greatly encouraged by an angelic visitation when they were young missionaries in the Andean highlands of Ecuador. They were living in a hostile environment, experiencing bitter opposition to their presence there. On occasions, small crowds would gather to hurl insults punctuated by stones at them. It was often difficult for Dr. Edmond and his wife to get the bare necessities of life, such as fruit and vegetables, or charcoal for the kitchen stove.

In the midst of these discouraging circumstances God sent an angel with words of strong encouragement to them in the form of a little Indian woman, dressed like the other Indian women in that area. Just as Raymond Edmond started to thank her for the extremely timely encouragement, the woman totally disappeared. Not a soul was in sight, though he looked in every possible place to locate her. That's when God let him know that He had not sent an earthly being at their time of need, but a ministering spirit, as described in Hebrews 1:14: "Are they not all ministering spirits sent forth to minister for those who will inherit salvation?"

Writing with His Finger

This method is simple, but very awesome. When God first gave us the Ten Commandments, the Bible clearly tells us in Exodus 31:18 that they were on two "tablets of stone, written with the finger of God." Then in Daniel 5:24, we read that the sovereign pronouncement of judgment concerning King Belshazzar, which predicted his death, was written on the wall of the banquet room by none other than the fingers of God's hand. "Then the fingers of the hand were sent from Him . . ."

There was another time when Jesus was dealing with the hypocrisy of the Scribes and Pharisees who were testing Him by bringing a woman caught in the act of adultery, to see whether Jesus would follow through with the Law of Moses by stoning her. Jesus simply stooped down and wrote on the ground with His finger. The content of whatever He wrote brought such conviction of sin to the accusers that they all split the scene, starting with the eldest (see John 8:6–9).

Rainbows

Rainbows are a permanent reminder to us of God's covenant to mankind that He will never again destroy the inhabitants of the earth by a flood, as He did in Noah's day, with the exception of Noah and his family (see Genesis 8:21–22).

Creation

God speaks through His creation, particularly through the heavens.

> *The heavens declare the glory of God;*
> *the skies proclaim the work of His hands.*
> *Day after day they pour forth speech;*
> *night after night they display knowledge.*
> *There is no speech or language*
> *where their voice is not heard.*
> *Their voice goes out into all the earth,*
> *their words to the ends of the world.* (Psalm 19:1–4 NIV)

And again,

> For since the creation of the world God's invisible qualities—
> His eternal power and divine nature—have been clearly seen,
> being understood from what has been made, so that men are
> without excuse. (Romans 1:20 NIV)

When we put the contents of these two verses together, we understand that every time anyone looks up into the skies and sees God's incredible handiwork, instinctively he or she knows there is a Creator, a supernatural Being at work behind it all. There is no such thing as an honest atheist.

A Pillar of Fire and a Pillar of Cloud

When God led the children of Israel out of Egypt on their journey into Canaan, He chose to direct them by sending a pillar of fire by night to give them light, and a pillar of cloud to lead them by day (see Exodus 13:21). They only moved on their journey when these visual manifestations from God moved forward.

A Consuming Fire

When God chose to show the children of Israel what His glory was like, which represents His character, He displayed it by turning on a consuming fire on the top of Mount Sinai, which all the people could see (see Exodus 24:17).

Supernatural Signs

Another way God communicates His will to us visually is through supernatural signs. Some people teach that it is a symptom of spiritual immaturity to ask God for a sign in order to be sure that we are in God's perfect will related to specific circumstances in our lives when we are seeking Him for directions.

However, the story in Isaiah 38 tells us that God took the initiative related to King Hezekiah's illness by telling the prophet Isaiah to tell Hezekiah that the sign or proof that God had heard his cry for healing, and had granted him fifteen more years of life, was that the sun would return ten degrees backward on the sundial (see v. 7). Wow! Think about it! God reversed the course of that planet, every square yard of which is constantly emitting 130,000 horsepower, to confirm His spoken word to an antlike creature of the dust, mortal man.

It is difficult to attach spiritual immaturity to the desire for signs after knowing about that one—especially since the One with ultimate maturity dreamed it up, authorized it, and executed it.

It is interesting that scientists have discovered that what we have always believed about that story because it is in God's Word is a scientifically proven fact. God does not need a scientist to prove anything that He has said or done. Scientists just keep finding out how accurate the Word of God is—more and more.

God gave Jonathan and his armor bearer a sign that they would win a battle in 1 Samuel 14:10, when they were outnumbered two to twenty. They won, big-time.

God gave Gideon three supernatural signs that he would win a battle (see Judges 6:21, 36–40; 7:13–15) when he and his little army of men were outnumbered, three hundred to the following mind-boggling statistics: "The Midianites and Amalekites, all the people of the East, were lying in the valley as numerous as locusts; and their camels were without number, as the sand by the seashore in multitude" (Judges 7:12).

Here's a word of caution. It is wiser to ask God to put the sign of *His* choosing into your mind. Do not dictate the sign to God. He will fulfill the sign He directs you to request.

Circumstances

Another visual means of God's communication to us is through circumstances that He either creates or allows. Many people take this method as one of the most obvious and reliable means of interpreting God's will, whereas I believe it should be one of the ways we should least expect Him to guide us. Circumstances can be the result of our poor choices; they can be engineered by satanic forces to keep us from God's highest purposes in our lives; they can be a means of God's testing us; or they can simply be the result of other people's presumptions, no matter how sincere they may be.

Therefore, circumstances are not necessarily sources of God's directions to us. The prophet Balaam is a classic example of a man to whom God was wanting to speak through circumstances, but failed to ask God the million-dollar question, "What is it, God, that You're trying to teach me?"

Many times we find ourselves in difficult situations, and like Balaam in Numbers chapter 22, we are hindered when we try to go somewhere or do something we want to do. In frustration, we may lash out verbally at the people (or in Balaam's case, at the animal) we perceive to have caused the trouble.

God will try again to get our attention. This time we may find ourselves, like Balaam, in physical pain. Balaam's foot was crushed against the wall when his donkey saw the angel of the Lord standing blocking the narrow path they were on. Balaam struck the donkey a second time. Finally the donkey quit trying to move and lay down on the ground (see Numbers 22:25–27).

When we still will not ask God if He is trying to say something to us about the wrong direction we are headed in, or about anything else that may be displeasing to Him in our lives, He has the ability to completely ground us. More than that, He will use any means He chooses to humble us so that we can learn to hear His voice.

God did the unthinkable. He caused the donkey to speak with a human voice (see Numbers 22:28). Even that phenomenon didn't cause Balaam to stop and think, *Maybe God is trying to get my attention. After all, this isn't exactly an everyday occurrence. Come to think of it, I've never thought or heard of such an amazing happening!* Instead, Balaam wanted to kill the faithful animal. Like many people who lash out in worse anger at the people around them because of thwarted plans, and blame them entirely.

Finally, God had pity on the innocent animal and opened the prophet's eyes. Balaam saw God's angel with a drawn sword in his hand and heard the rebuke from headquarters heaven about Balaam's perverseness (see Numbers 22:31–32).

Although in this instance God was using difficult circumstances to speak to Balaam, we must not presume that a string of favorable circumstances is necessarily a sign from God that we are on the right track in relation to His will and purposes, although they can be.

The Urim and Thummim

Another visual method of God revealing His mind to His people is through the Urim and Thummim: "Also put the Urim and Thummim in the breastpiece, so they may be over Aaron's heart whenever he enters the presence of the LORD. Thus Aaron will always bear the means of making decisions for the Israelites over his heart before the LORD" (Exodus 28:30 NIV).

We also read, "He is to stand before Eleazar the priest, who will obtain decisions for him by inquiring of the Urim before the LORD. At his command he and the entire community of the Israelites will go out, and at his command they will come in" (Numbers 27:21 NIV). The Bible is silent as to how the Urim and Thummim were used by God to give directions to the Israelites through the priest, but it is clear that God spoke in this way during Old Testament times.

Casting Lots

Casting lots was a visual method of obtaining God's direction when the children of Israel were being allotted their inherited lands (see Joshua 8:8–10). It was also the method the apostles used when they were asking God who was to replace Judas after his death, and Matthias was chosen (see Acts 1:23–26).

God Speaks Through Our Hearing

Direct Conversation into Our Minds

When God speaks into our minds, His voice is inaudible to our outer ears, but clear to the inner ear of our spirits. "My sheep hear My voice, and I know them, and they follow Me"

(John 10:27). We frequently read in the Scriptures that "God spoke to Moses" or "God spoke to Abraham" or "God spoke to Noah." The list is endless, and we have no problem believing that, so why should we not believe that it is just as natural for God to speak to us?

We should note that He does not promise to speak to casual inquirers, only to diligent seekers. "But without faith it is impossible to please Him, for he who comes to God must believe that He is, and that He is a rewarder of those who diligently seek Him" (Hebrews 11:6).

There is nothing casual about God's relationship with us and He does not expect us to be casual with Him. And besides, when we see Him face-to-face in all His awesome holiness and blazing glory, it will seem incredible to us that we ever had a casual thought in relation to Him.

You may be thinking, *okay, so I believe God is committed to talking to me, but how will I know I'll have the ability to hear what He's saying? After all, He's in a league of His own and I'm just an ant-like creature of the dust.*

God has that base covered. As I've said before, He says, as He describes Himself as a shepherd, ". . . and His sheep hear His voice; and He calls His own sheep by name [how wonderfully personal] and leads them out. And when He brings out His own sheep, He goes before them; and the sheep follow Him, for they know His voice" (John 10:34). If there is a room full of mothers and a yard full of children outside playing, when one mother calls her child's name, how many children look up? Only one. That one's name may be Johnny and there may be three Johnnys in the yard, but still only one looks up. Why? Because that particular Johnny knows the sound of his mother's voice.

So it is with God. The more we spend time alone with Him, listening quietly to His voice, the more familiar it will become to the ear of our spirits. It's that simple. Don't complicate it through unbelief or cynicism.

I was in Lausanne, Switzerland, at YWAM's training school as a Bible teacher when Don Stephens, the school director at that time, knocked on the door of my room in the hotel YWAM owns. He had come to share with me that there was a castle in Munich, Germany, that was for sale. YWAM needed training facilities in Germany, so he asked me to seek God with him to see if we were to purchase it.

He knew what I knew. We had no money whatsoever for even the down payment. I said, "Sure. I will seek God. I'll let you know as soon as He speaks to me." He left. For some reason I chose to sit on the floor. After resisting the voice of demons in the name of the Lord Jesus Christ, should they have been anywhere around, I asked the uncomplicated question, "Lord, do we buy the castle?" I waited and listened.

Very simply and quietly I heard in my spirit one word: "Yes." This was accompanied by a deep-seated conviction and the peace I had long since come to recognize as God's confirming signal. Without delay, I shared my answer with Don. It confirmed what God had spoken to him, and we started the process of submitting our impressions to Loren Cunningham, the international director of YWAM. He was in another country at the time, but did exactly what we did and received the same impression we received from God. The rest is history. Through a series of remarkable miracles, we bought a castle. I well remember thinking how delightfully uncomplicated the ways of God are, compared to the ways of men. There were no drawn-out committee meetings, no talking about the pros and cons, no discussions about how and from where would we ever get the finances.

You may be thinking, *Well, I can't relate to hearing God's voice in relation to purchasing a castle.* I understand. So, how about this one? Jim and I were back in New Zealand where I had been speaking at a conference. It was the day before we returned to our home in Los Angeles, and we were out on a prayer walk in a beautiful, big park. I noticed a young man walking ahead of us. Immediately the Holy Spirit said to me, "He's in trouble; go and speak to him."

As I approached the man, the Holy Spirit gave me understanding about what to say. Smiling, I gently said, "Excuse me, sir, my husband and I are out walking in this park, praying for this nation. I felt impressed by God to tell you that God knows all about your problems. He has the power to solve them and the love for you that longs to solve them. Does that make any sense to you?" He said it made perfect sense to him. He then shared that he was physically sick, afraid of a recent medical diagnosis, out of work, was lonely, and that although he had been a churchgoer, he was considering giving up on Christianity altogether.

While Jim prayed silently, I expressed sincere, compassionate concern for this man's needs and asked him if I could pray for him. He gratefully consented. I prayed in faith for the healing of his body, and that God would speak to him from the Bible and get him employment. I then told him that we lived in California, that I had been speaking at a conference nearby which was held in a very vital church in his area, and strongly recommended that he should start attending. I assured him that God would meet his need for friendship and fellowship among those believers, and the needed employment might possibly come from his sharing that need with them. I continued to tell him that God loved and cared enough for him to send us from the United States to deliver this personal message from the Lord to him. The man was deeply touched, expressed sincere gratitude, and assured us that he would follow through on everything that had been shared.

God has put people around you with whom He wants you to share His love in an equally simple and effective way. When we have a burdened heart to reach the lost, God will alert us to the prepared hearts and, in His faithfulness, tell us exactly what we're to say and when to say it.

Trust Him.

With an Audible Voice

He did so at Saul of Tarsus' conversion in Acts 9:4–6. He did the same thing for an Asian young woman named Nita Edwards after she had been lying in bed for a year, totally paralyzed from an accident, with her body steadily deteriorating. She could not even speak. When she was totally alone, God spoke audibly and told her He was going to raise her up and make her a witness for Him in Asia. Then He spoke the day, the exact date, and month. I tell the whole incredible story in Chapter 10 of my book *Some of the Ways of God in Healing*.

A friend of mine was twenty-eight years old when, at the invitation of a friend, she went to a home Bible study meeting, and for the first time in her life heard the way of salvation. The next day during lunchtime, when everyone else had gone out of the office building where she worked, she sat alone weighing the implications of committing her life to the Lord Jesus Christ. To her amazement she heard an audible voice behind her, clearly stating "I will never let you down." She immediately checked her office and two outer offices to see who had entered. There was no one. God was audibly confirming His written Word: "I will never leave you nor forsake you" (Hebrews 13:5).

That woman took God at His word that day, gave her whole life to Christ, and became a wonderful woman of God influencing many other lives.

The Gifts of the Holy Spirit

You will find a list of the gifts of the Holy Spirit in 1 Corinthians 12:8–11. They are:

- word of wisdom

- word of knowledge

- faith

- gifts of healings

- working of miracles

- prophecy

- discerning of spirits

- different kinds of tongues

- interpretation of tongues

I will illustrate the word of knowledge. The prophet Elisha had the gift of a word of knowledge operating when his servant Gehazi lied to Naaman, the general of the Assyrian army. Gehazi said Elisha wanted money and clothing after Elisha had just refused the gifts. The lie was supernaturally revealed to Elisha by God's Spirit, and judgment came to Gehazi (see 2 Kings 5:26–27).

The same gift operated through the apostle Paul in Acts 5, when Ananias and his wife, Sapphira, lied and withheld some of the money they received after selling some property instead of obeying God and giving all the money to God's work. The judgment of God came on them both, as through the gift of prophecy Paul declared it would. They died.

The gifts of the Spirit are wonderful tools to aid us in our differing ministry functions. The operation of the revelation gifts can save multiplied hours of counseling people in need.

A woman had responded to an appeal given in our church for people to come forward who needed help spiritually. As I was listening to her complex tale of woe, the Holy Spirit revealed to me through a word of knowledge that the cause of her many problems was basically resentment toward her mother. When I spoke it out, she immediately acknowledged this was correct and I was able to take her through the Biblical steps to complete forgiveness, which led to her freedom in other areas of her life. I have shared these important steps on fogiveness in Chapter 7 in my book *Some of the Ways of God in Healing* from YWAM Publishing.

God exhorts us in 1 Corinthians 14:1 that we are to "pursue love, and desire spiritual gifts." That order is of utmost importance. The power of the love of God is the strongest force in the universe to motivate people to make the right choices, which brings about the greatest changes in their lives. Satanic forces can counterfeit some of the power of God, but they can never counterfeit the love of God because it is based in humility. Our motive in operating the gifts of the Spirit should always be to glorify God.

Immediately after God gives us the wonderful promise in Psalm 32:8 that He will instruct us and teach us the way we should go and that He will counsel us with His eye upon us, we have a warning. He tells us not to be like the horse that runs ahead or the mule that lags behind.

In this regard, it is important for us to understand that there is a difference between the moving of the Holy Spirit in us, and the moment for discharging or seeing the fulfillment of that movement. There can be seconds, minutes, hours, days, weeks, months, or years between the movement and the moment.

I'll illustrate in relation to the gifts of the Holy Spirit. A mature man of God whom I knew well received a strong prophetic word of warning about a false prophet who would show up. He had no idea to whom that word referred. As he waited on God, understanding came that this spiritual leader was to refrain from saying anything at that time. Days, weeks, and months passed and still no release. Then one night, three months after the prophecy had been given to him, he was released to speak it out to a group of mature Christians. The timing proved to be perfect. The false prophet was soon exposed and dealt with.

When we are in a group of other Christians and we are stirred by the Holy Spirit to operate any of the gifts of the Spirit as previously mentioned, we should always wait and check with God to make sure we have the right moment for God's movement. In His faithfulness, God will make His timing known.

If you are not sure, then submit your impressions to a trustworthy spiritual leader and let that person help you. In fact, submitting your impressions to a spiritual leader first, before you move out in the operation of the gifts of the Spirit, is a safe and wise practice.

We don't need to have a change of voice or put on a preachy tone to move in the things of the Spirit. There is really no need for any embellishments. We should speak naturally and distinctly. The less attention that is drawn to us, the better.

We never need to announce to others the ministry function God has given us nor the supernatural gifts with which He has graced us. As we make it a way of life to walk in obedience to revealed truth and the promptings of the Holy Spirit, others will be used of God to recognize our ministries and giftings.

If we feel the need for self-promotion at any time, from God's perspective, we are not ready to function in the area in which we're trying to operate. I have always said, "If God doesn't open the door of opportunity in which I'm to minister, I don't want to go through that door."

Music and Poetry

God speaks through the ministry of music in song and poetry. Times without number God has used music and songs in powerful ways to get His truths across when people have resisted His voice in other ways.

The Book of Psalms is a classic example. The Psalms are full of expressions of our hearts to God and the responsive expressions of God's heart to us. During Bible times, the Psalms were set to music and sung, and are some of the most powerful and precious portions of the Scripture.

Other People

God speaks through people He specifically sends to a person or a group. He used Abigail, a wise woman, to warn King David of hasty, presumptuous actions he was about to take (see 1 Samuel 25:23–31).

God used the prophet Nathan to expose King David's hidden sin of adultery with Bathsheba (see 2 Samuel 12:1–12).

If we do not know the character of the person, or that the person has a proven ministry, when he or she brings what may be called a "word from the Lord" to us, we should not automatically receive the message. Rather, we need to weigh the contents in the light of God's Word, God's character, and God's ways, and heed any checks in our spirit that may accordingly come to us from the Holy Spirit.

If there is a definite witness in our spirits that a message is from the Lord through another person, we should receive it in humility and with gratitude. If in doubt, ask the Holy Spirit to show us the source and believe He will direct us.

The story of the young prophet and the older prophet in 1 Kings 13 is a strong warning to keep obeying God's voice and not to be sidetracked by the voice of man when it conflicts with God's instructions.

The Animal Kingdom

We have already seen from the story of the prophet Balaam in Numbers 22:28–30 that God humbled and rebuked Balaam through causing his donkey to speak to him with the voice of a human being.

Obviously, God can use any means He chooses to communicate to us—anywhere, at any time, without having to give us any explanation. He's *God*, the ruling, reigning monarch of the universe. We bow to His supreme sovereignty and majesty. God's business corporation is *unlimited*.

Testimonies

God spoke to Peter when his brother Andrew told him about meeting Jesus and the impact that He had on Andrew's life. As a result Peter became a disciple of Jesus (see John 1:40–42).

God spoke to the people in the city of Samaria when a woman with a seamy past had an encounter with the Lord Jesus at lunchtime by a well and testified to them about her dramatically changed life. Many of the Samaritans subsequently believed in Him as the Messiah (see John 4:5–42).

God spoke to the people in the Decapolis (a region of ten cities) near the Jordan River through the testimony of a man whom Jesus freed from a legion of demonic spirits. Considerably more lives were impacted through this power encounter with the living Christ (see Luke 8:26–39). Statistics prove that more people are brought to faith in Christ and discipled through one-on-one personal testimony than any other way.

God Speaks Through Impressions to Our Spirits

A Strong Conviction and Peace

Regardless of what other ways God speaks to us, every method should be accompanied by a strong assurance in our spirits and a deep, settled peace in our hearts and minds that God has spoken. ". . . the mind controlled by the Spirit is life and peace" (Romans 8:6 NIV).

If you do not experience this state of mind, do not act on

impressions you receive. Wait, and seek God's face again. This method is also totally valid on its own. If you have nothing else but a strong witness in your spirit, accompanied by the peace of God, you can rest assured God has revealed His will to you. Remember, "Let the peace of Christ rule in your hearts" (Colossians 3:15 NIV).

Jim and I were once staying overnight in London with a few other leaders after being at a YWAM leadership conference in Switzerland. Airline seats were available for us to get a flight home to Los Angeles on either the eighth or the tenth of October. As we sought God for His timing, I had an impression that we were to depart on the tenth.

However, in Jim's daily reading of the Scriptures there was a verse that totally identified with our circumstances, saying the exact opposite: "On the eighth day he sent the people away; and they blessed the king, and went to their tents joyful and glad of heart for all the good that the LORD had done for His servant David, and for Israel His people" (1 Kings 8:66).

Naturally we were strongly arrested by this verse which seemingly gave us a tailor-made answer. But we also noticed that there was an absence of that deep conviction and peace that accompanies the voice of the Lord. What were we to do?

The most important thing to tell you at this point is that we relaxed in the Lord's presence, worshiped Him, and thanked Him that as our loving heavenly Father He would clearly make known to us whether He was giving to us remarkable guidance through His Word that the correct date was the eighth, or if He was speaking into our spirits that we were to depart on the tenth. We made sure we had died to all human reasonings and desires and that satanic forces were silenced in Jesus' name.

We asked for two things. First, that God would direct both of our minds toward whichever date was right and speak that into our spirits. Second, that a deep peace and conviction would accompany those impressions. After a time of quiet listening, when we both indicated that we were ready to share, Jim spoke first and said, "I've heard from the Lord. It's the tenth. There's no question left in my mind about what we're to do. I wouldn't even consider going on the eighth now." God had confirmed the same thing to me. The point of this illustration is that no matter how many Bible verses fit your circumstances, or how many signs and wonders you may be given, if there is an absence of that deep peace from the Holy Spirit that assures you God has spoken, don't act. Wait on the Lord until His peace rules in your heart in relation to the decision. I cannot say too strongly that, basically, the condition of our hearts determines the correctness of our guidance. "For as many as are led by the Spirit of God, these are sons of God" (Romans 8:14).

The more our lives are under the direct control of the Holy Spirit, the more readily we will be able to discern and interpret the quickening of the Spirit. The following five conditions need to be fulfilled on a daily basis to ensure this condition:

1. Having a totally yielded will to God (see 2 Corinthians 5:15)

2. Asking God to convict of any sin, repenting, and making any restitution that He should require (see Proverbs 28:13)

3. Asking for the Holy Spirit's control and receiving it by faith (see Ephesians 5:18)

4. Resisting the enemy in the name of the Lord Jesus Christ (see James 4:7)

5. Obeying revealed truth and the promptings of the Holy Spirit (see Acts 5:32)

The Promptings of the Holy Spirit

This method can be interpreted as a nudge in our spirits that God wants to get our attention or to remind us of something.

Numbers of times when I have been teaching God's Word, I have sensed this nudge and have stopped speaking and quietly listened to the voice of God. His explanations and directions have been different, with significant results in relation to the many and varied audiences to whom I have spoken.

The Constraints or Restraints of the Holy Spirit

This method and the previous method can only be experienced when we are totally submitted to the control of the Holy Spirit in the fear of the Lord, which releases us from the fear of other people.

I had been speaking for about eight minutes at a conference of thousands of people in the USA when I sensed an increasingly strong restraint of the Holy Spirit. I stopped speaking and sought God for the explanation. As I waited in silence, God revealed to me that a large number of the audience did not believe that the message I was giving titled "Jesus, the Master Soul Winner" could be applied to their lives. I spoke this out and called the people to repent of this sin of unbelief, giving them time to follow through. Then the Holy Spirit released me to give the rest of the message. The atmosphere became as different as night from day and the people were then able to receive and apply the word of the Lord to their lives.

Another time when I was speaking at a church in Latvia, a Baltic State, I experienced the strongest constraint of the Spirit when I came to the point of the joy of the Lord in whatever message I gave that day. Every time I tried to get on to the next point, the Holy Spirit compelled me to speak some more on the joy of the Lord. This went on for more than twenty minutes. Later, one of the Latvian spiritual leaders told me that the joy of the Lord was foreign to them and that God had targeted a nerve of need among His precious people.

Another time I had received an invitation from a pastor friend to hold a series of meetings at his church. I sought God and He said, "Yes." The pastor had asked me to start on a Monday night and go through to the Sunday night, but whenever I sought God about this schedule, I became aware of a constraint in my spirit about speaking at the Sunday services.

God's direction did not make a grain of sense to my human reasoning. The largest number of people always attended the two Sunday services and I was available on that date. When I shared my impressions by phone with the pastor, he too had zero understanding, so we agreed that I would go and speak from Monday through Friday night and keep seeking God throughout the week. I did, although the pastor was urging me to continue through Sunday.

Because the whole thing seemed so illogical, I actually sought God three different times, and each time He spoke the same answer into my spirit: "Return to your home on Saturday morning."

That was it, despite the pastor's comments on how very

strange it all seemed to him. I assured him that it wasn't all that strange to me because on many occasions God had told me to do things that were contrary to my human reasonings and/or desires, and every time, through obedience to His voice, the outcome was perfect.

I told the pastor my mission at his church would be completed on Friday night. The next day my husband phoned me to say that a young spiritual leader whom I had never met called and left a message that he felt it was important to spend some time with me. He explained that he had only partial understanding of God's purposes, and that he was coming to Los Angeles from another country and would only be available for a few hours on Saturday morning before he had to fly out again. The young leader had no idea of my itinerary, but said he would do anything to meet with me anywhere.

The Holy Spirit let me know in a hurry that this was the reason for sending me home. It was obviously more important to God for me to spend time with this little-known young man than to speak to many hundreds of people in two church services. I took the first flight home on Saturday morning and was able to have quality time with him, which had significant implications for his life and mine.

It was a crisis time directionally for his life. Later, he was God's instrument to open up strategic doors of ministry in an overseas country for me. That visit was the start of a lifelong close friendship. His name is Floyd McClung. After serving in a senior leadership position in YWAM for many years, he became the senior pastor of the Metro Christian Fellowship. He is a missionary statesman of the first order and the author of a number of vital books.

How many times do we miss the will of God through insensitivity to the restraints of the Holy Spirit, and because of our inability to understand God's directions with our finite minds? All too often, I'm afraid.

God has warned us by telling us that "'My thoughts are not your thoughts, nor are your ways My ways,' says the LORD. 'For as the heavens are higher than the earth, so are My ways higher than your ways, and My thoughts than your thoughts'" (Isaiah 55:8–9).

We will never experience intimate friendship with God until we have learned to be obedient to the constraints and restraints of the Holy Spirit in matters small and large.

By God's Physical Touch

Psalm 147:5 says, "His understanding is infinite" (or "unsearchable"). The following story illustrates this verse.

A spiritual leader was sharing with me in her home about how God had fulfilled Isaiah 43:2 to her in a marvelous way. God says in this Scripture that when we walk through the fire we will not be burned.

She had just come through a very painful experience of being misjudged and hurt by spiritual leaders, but she said, holding out her arm to me, "Look, Joy, I haven't been burned or even scorched." That was her way of saying that God's supernatural grace was upon her under very difficult relationship circumstances.

I felt God's compassion toward her and prayed for her. We were completely alone. When I finished, she told me that when I was praying, she felt a strong hand grip her arm. Her first reaction was annoyance that someone had intruded on our privacy. But when she opened her eyes, there was no one in sight. She then knew it was the hand of God touching her as a sign of His loving encouragement.

Impressions or Senses

An impression or sense of the Holy Spirit's leading can come in a flash of understanding related to circumstances in our lives that have been previously perplexing. An impression can also come in the form of a revelation of truth from God's Word, or a truth that someone has shared of which we had little or no previous understanding. We may have prayed like David in Psalm 43:3, "Send forth Your light and Your truth, let them guide me . . ." (NIV). and suddenly the light switch goes on and we "see" the truth. It's like a time bomb. It explodes later.

That is why we do not need to worry about remembering a lot of truth we may have heard at any one time. If we believe it and receive it, and are ready to act upon it, God will have the time bomb of revelation explode just when we need it.

The many ways God uses to speak to us are relatively unimportant. We do not need to make a big deal out of any of them. I have only shared them so that we can better understand and recognize them when God uses any of them to communicate His loving heart to us.

The big thing is, *who He is*, who speaks to us. The more time we spend studying God's character and ways, the easier we will recognize His precious voice.

The next section of this book will provide some answers to many questions you may have as to why you have not heard from God after lots of earnest seeking.

Many Reasons Why God
Delays Answers

Tests and Purposes Connected
With Delays

$\mathcal{P}$erhaps you have fulfilled all the conditions for hearing God's voice the best you know how and still have not heard what you need to hear. Maybe you are perplexed and somewhat frustrated. Could be that you have even given up seeking God for answers. You could be thinking that all this teaching on divine guidance apparently works for others, but it sure does not work for you. I have spoken with people in that condition. Worse yet, you may have decided to give up on the whole business of following the Lord because in your thinking, you did your part in seeking God and obeying what you believe was His voice and the outcome was not what you anticipated.

You expected 2+2 to equal 4, and you ended up in your reckoning with 2+2 making 27! In your confusion and disappointment, you may have blamed God for not coming through and doing His part. So now you are confused and feel He can't be trusted. Maybe you told others that God told you He would do such-and-such a thing at a specific time. It did not happen, so you feel stupid and embarrassed.

If you can identify with any of the above, I'm so glad you are reading this section because I believe God is about to give you understanding according to His character and ways from His Word. Let's take an honest look at some of the reasons that our just, wise and all-knowing God delays answers to our prayers.

First a word of caution. When seeking God for answers,

make the questions simple, and ask only one question at a time. This is very important. Anything else only produces confusion. Not that God can't handle more than one question at a time, but because the answer to one question may well be different from the answer to another question when we put them together as a request. So God waits until we separate them before answering us.

1. First, we may have asked the wrong question. It could be an unwise one, or it may be a good question, but one that is not asked in the proper order or timing. For example, it is unwise to ask God if we're going to suffer and be persecuted as a martyr. If we are, God will prepare us ahead of time by taking the initiative and telling us when He sees we are sufficiently spiritually mature to handle that knowledge. Jesus said to His disciples, "I still have many things to say to you, but you cannot bear them now" (John 16:12).

2. If you are still not getting an answer, you need to ask God whether there is something more important in His order of things for your life that He wants to tell you first. Simply ask Him to drop that question into your mind and trust Him. He will. He is faithful and wants to help you.

3. Or, we could be asking God questions related to other people's lives that are none of our business.

4. It is also important to ask God to reveal to us any points of disobedience in our lives. He often waits for us to be obedient to previous orders He has given us before He can trust us with more.

5. It could be that we are out of order in regard to the lines of authority over us, and that it's not our place of responsibility to be asking the questions.

6. On the other hand, there may be another person or other people who should be added to those making the inquiry of the Lord, before He will answer. We need to check out these possibilities in God's presence as simple, but important, explanations as to why God is silent.

I had been invited to seek God for answers over important issues related to the extension of God's Kingdom with a group of spiritual leaders of an international missionary organization. After listening in silence for some time to hear God's voice concerning the first item on the agenda, it became apparent to each one of us that God was not speaking. The group was puzzled and had no understanding.

I asked if there was anyone else on the leadership team who happened to be absent from the meeting. One of the directors said, "Yes, my wife." I suggested that her absence could be the missing factor. As soon as she arrived and sought God with us, the Holy Spirit released the answers to all our questions. Divine order is very important to God.

7. We may have consciously or unconsciously been dictating to God the method with which we want Him to speak to us.

I remember hearing the testimony of an intelligent young man who was following a scientific career, when God stirred his heart about being trained for ministry service with the Wycliffe Bible Translators. This organization translates the Bible for people groups of the world who do not yet have it in their native language.

Wycliffe was about to have a training course at this particular time and the young man, David, needed to know God's clear direction as to whether he was to make application to attend. David sought God diligently day after day for God to speak to him from his daily reading of the Scriptures. God was silent. David was desperate for an answer because he would have to wait another six months to go into training if he did not make this particular course.

David finally told God that he would take any method God chose to speak to him from His Word, even if it was the one he had been told was unreliable. He felt cornered, but he took his Bible in his hands, closed his eyes and reverently asked God to speak to him, reminding God of the urgency of his situation and explaining that he only wanted to do God's will as his entire future depended upon this pivotal decision—either a scientist or a missionary in who-knows-where!

He opened his Bible and his eyes immediately fell on the following verses, "'Whom will he teach knowledge? And whom will he make to understand the message? Those just weaned from milk? Those just drawn from the breasts? For precept must be upon precept, precept upon precept, line upon line, line upon line, here a little, there a little. For with stammering lips and another tongue He will speak to this people" (Isaiah 28:9–11). Verse thirteen is partially a repeat of verse ten.

Nothing in all the Bible could more accurately describe the ministry of translating the Scriptures word-by-word into foreign languages. David bowed his head and heart before our Sovereign God and thanked Him for speaking in a way that left him in no doubt as to the course of his future. In one moment, God had also dispelled his reservations and fears about God using that particular method to speak to him from His Word. That was thirty years ago, during which time David has become a veteran, effective missionary leader to the Mexican people.

8. Another reason God delays answers is that, because of the method God wants to use to speak to us, other circumstances may have to take place before He can. The perplexities surrounding this point can be numerous, depending upon how many other people's choices God is having to deal with, that affect His answers to our questions. We rest in God's omniscience, wisdom, and faithfulness to give us our directions as soon as He is able in the light of this truth.

9. There are times when we have fulfilled all the conditions to hear God's voice and still He is silent, so we bow to God's sovereignty and trust Him to come through on time. He is never too late.

I will illustrate from my experience with two mature YWAM leaders who had been living by these principles of divine guidance for years. They had come to me individually for counsel during a YWAM leadership conference. Both of them had received stirrings in their spirits from God that there was going to come a change in the location of their sphere of ministry within our mission. After diligently seeking God for specific directions over a considerable period of time neither of them had a clue. And neither one knew that the other was in the same dilemma; only I knew that.

God had given both of them the understanding that the guidance would be released at the leadership conference. I asked them both separately (as I was counseling them individually) to get alone with the Lord and make certain they were fulfilling all the conditions of hearing God's voice I have taught in this book.

They did their homework thoroughly and reported that there was still no breakthrough. When I asked the Lord for understanding He showed me clearly that there were factors related to others that had to take place before God could give them their new directions, and assured them that the holdup had nothing to do with them. They were relieved and encouraged.

Two days later, their leader, Loren Cunningham, called them separately into his office and said that while he was in prayer, God surprised him by speaking to him about each of these leaders at different times, and giving him clear understanding that they were to move to different locations. One was to go to a different nation. The names of the places were also released to Loren.

Loren then submitted these impressions to each one of these people, asking them to seek the Lord what He would say and to report back. God *immediately* confirmed to these leaders in remarkable ways that those places were indeed exactly where they were to relocate. I had sessions of great rejoicing with both of them separately. God's ways are not our ways, in fact, He says they are "past finding out" (Job 9:10).

10. It is important to note that in these cases, God gave the answers first to a leader in a ministry position of seniority over them, not under them. And, in turn, that leader submitted his impressions back to the staff under his authority for them to allow God to speak to them individually. This was not a dictatorial setup. Loren made sure that they heard from God for themselves before releasing them to their new ministry assignments.

I know of an instance in which a spiritual leader asked others under his authority to seek God for direction concerning that leader's need for guidance before going to the leader over him. This resulted in much confusion because they were operating contrary to divine order. Clarity only came when there was humbling of spirit and repentance before God and man, and the one needing direction operated within God's divine order.

11. Another example is that God may choose to speak to us from our daily reading of the Scriptures, and we have not reached that particular portion yet in the sequence of the pattern of our reading. Hang in there, friend. The answer is on the way.

The Lord once spoke into my spirit, telling me to give a sum of money to a missionary organization. I didn't have the money, so I said, "If You give it to me in some way, I'll certainly pass it on." That was the only way I knew how to be obedient. I continued to say to God, "You know I have no way to obtain this money." Then He said, "You have your little car. Sell it and use the money."

My response as a willing bond-slave of the Lord Jesus was a simple "Okay, Lord, that's it." Because the car was a small, old, beaten-up "bomb" I was glad that the responsibility of selling it would be on the Lord!

This car was my only means of transportation in the large city where I lived, and I relied on it frequently to get me to my speaking engagements. It was also necessary for getting food supplies for our family of four, as we lived at the bottom of hills which were at a distance from the stores.

Because of these implications of selling the car without having another one I asked God to confirm to me from His Word if my impressions were from Him. After diligently seeking Him, I had no answer. The next day, the same silence. The third day in my daily devotional Bible reading, the answer came like a personal E-mail from God, "Sell your possessions, and give alms" (Luke 12:33 RSV). Nothing could be clearer. Hallelujah!

The benefit of being an obedient bond-slave of Jesus is that all the responsibility for the consequences rest on Him, so I didn't feel anything but fascinating anticipation of seeing how God would work things out for me. I revel in the adventure of hearing and obeying God's voice.

My next inquiry of God was, "For how much am I to sell the car?" Speaking into my spirit, He named a price, and I thanked Him. My husband asked our local car dealer friend what price we should ask for my car and, unhesitatingly, our friend named a figure. I hadn't said a word to my husband the amount God had spoken to me, but our friend's price was exactly the same amount! More rejoicing.

I kept thinking that the greatest miracle in all this would be that anyone would want to buy the little old "bomb." But as soon as Jim mentioned to one of the men who worked with him that the car was for sale, the man said that our price was exactly what he wanted to pay for a car for his son, and bought it. No sweat.

This was a Friday evening. For the next three days we were at a conference and I didn't need my car. The very next Tuesday morning at 11:00 A.M., I had a phone call from a friend asking if she could come to my home for spiritual counseling. I explained that I had mountains of housework needing to be done, and that a visit was not convenient, but I would seek God and call her back. The Holy Spirit said, "Take her." So that was my answer.

During the course of our conversation, she recommended that I should attend some vital meetings that week across town. When I explained that I had no transportation, she expressed amazement and then burst out saying, "So you're the one to whom I'm to loan my car for an indefinite period!" She explained that all throughout the three-day conference we had both attended, she was puzzled about why God never answered her repeated inquiry as to what she was to do with her car, as He had called her to do missionary work on an island where she would have no use for her vehicle. Believe it or not, she was going to work with the same organization to which God had told me to give the money!

I gave up a little old car only to be provided with a much better one. "No good thing will He withhold from those who walk uprightly" (Psalm 84:11).

12. When seeking God together in a team situation, God can withhold an answer from one of the members because of the following reasons:

- Maybe because of undealt-with pride because of the clarity and frequency with which one person hears God's voice

- Maybe because God wants to especially encourage one or more of the team by giving them the answer and withholding it from another

- Possibly teaching each of us to be humble and willing to receive direction from the Lord through others, without being irresponsible

- Possibly teaching us to be dependent on the Lord through others for the purposes of having closer fellowship with them

I was teaching in Switzerland at a YWAM staff conference at the hotel YWAM owns as a training center. It was a Saturday and I had been seeking God at length for the message I was to give that evening. The Creator and C.E.O. of the heavenly realm was silent.

As I sought Him for understanding, He brought the names of three people to my mind and said, "Go to each of their rooms and ask them to pray for the message to be released to you." I obeyed. Each person had the same reaction. They were delighted to have this prayer participation and that God had singled them out for this purpose. It was a precious, although brief, time of further bonding our hearts together. Immediately after I returned to my room the message was released to me. It was also a reminder to me of my codependency upon others in the Body of Christ.

Now for a word of caution. We can find verses in the Bible to correspond with just about anything we want to do if we search long enough. But that is not what I am teaching. I am sharing about the various ways God quickens His Word to us by the power of the Holy Spirit and shows us verses that give us counsel, direction, conviction of sin, revelation of truth, and confirmation for specific needs as we seek Him.

- Here's another illustration related to God's timing in speaking to two people from His Word. In 1971, God had stirred Jim's and my heart in relation to leaving our home in New Zealand and living in Los Angeles, California, to become full-time missionaries with YWAM. The entire future of our family of four was at stake. We dared not make a mistake.

We asked God for scriptural confirmation if we were hearing Him correctly. In my normal course of Bible reading one morning, the Holy Spirit strongly quickened to me Genesis 12:1 and 5. "Now the LORD had said to Abram: 'Get out of your country, from your family and from your father's house, to a land that I will show you' . . . Then Abraham took Sarai his wife . . . and all their possessions that they had gathered, and the people whom they had acquired . . . and they departed to go to the land of Canaan."

This was strong confirmation that God was directing us. But as Jim is the head of the home, he naturally longed for God to give him something equally confirming from His Word and was puzzled as to why it seemed to be withheld. Two weeks later, in the normal course of Jim's daily Bible reading, the exact same instances as are related in Genesis 12 are recorded in Acts 7:2–4. They were strongly impressed upon his spirit and he knew that God was giving him the requested confirmation.

Again, don't be discouraged that your answer hasn't come yet. It's on the way in God's way and time.

- At times, God delays answering us but will in time, not only answer us but often give us an explanation of the delay.

There was a time in Daniel's life when he had to wait for twenty-one days before God answered his request because of strong spiritual warfare between satanic forces and God's warring angels (see Daniel 10:10–14). In God's sovereignty He can also withhold an answer and not give us an explanation for the delay.

- In Jeremiah 42:7, Jeremiah waited ten days before receiving the word of the Lord to give to the people without having understanding why.

On one of the occasions when Moses went up Mount Sinai at the call of God, He chose not to speak one word to Moses until six days had passed—without explanation (see Exodus 24:16). Many Christians give up seeking God if He does not answer them in six minutes!

- Sometimes God causes us to wait for His answers because He has purposes to be worked out in the lives of others first. Perhaps there are things God is in the process of teaching them that are connected with our lives.

I had been alone seeking God all day as to the message I was to give at the close of a Methodist renewal conference that evening without receiving a thing. When the married couple picked me up from the hotel to drive me to the conference, I mentioned that I didn't yet have the word of the Lord, was not uptight about it, but would be grateful if they would pray for God to release it to me. We had a ten-minute drive before arriving at the convention center with two thousand people in attendance. My heavy briefcase was loaded with the many messages God had given me because I didn't know which one was needed.

Instantly, the woman (who had only been converted a few years) started to pray for me, and the Holy Spirit spoke to me the title of the message, "Knowing God." When she had finished the prayer I told her what had happened and expressed gratitude. She was utterly amazed and incredulously stammered out, "You mean my prayer alone released the message? I've heard it called inter– inter- I can't remember the right terminology—what is it . . . ?" I assured her I understood and said the word was *intercession*.

Immediately I had understanding of why God had withheld the knowledge of that message from me. It was to show this new convert the powerful ministry of praying for others into which God was leading her. She was encouraged "out of her socks," to say the least. God is faithful and wise.

- Perhaps God withholds an answer from us because He is testing the reaction of someone near us, should the answer be other than what they would choose. He could be trying to bring them to a new place of relinquishing us and themselves into God's hands for whatever new purposes He has for both lives.

- Also, if others knew first what God had spoken to us in a group situation, they could be tempted to follow our directions instead of getting their directions from the Lord firsthand.

- Another reason for a delay is that another or others may need to take responsibility with us in seeking God for an answer on a particular issue. For example, my husband, Jim, and I operate totally as a team. We're like the knife and fork. "You can't have one without the other," as the old song says. We have a united ministry. We are equal in importance, but different in function and ministry giftings. Generally speaking, if one of us seeks God alone, God remains silent until we take the responsibility together. However, if we are separated from one another and need immediate answers from the Lord, we trust each other to get God's mind and to act accordingly.

- God may be withholding the answer from us because others in leadership have delayed in fulfilling their responsibility to ask us to fulfill some ministry assignment related to a particular time frame. Do not act presumptuously. Ask God to act on the leadership in relation to us so that we can know God's will for the time frame with which we are concerned.

When the Next Move Is God's

Now for those of you who have received no answers over a long period of time of seeking God, having fulfilled all the conditions, here's my counsel: put Psalm 35:5 into action. Stop inquiring and commit the matter into God's hands. The Hebrew word for "commit" means "to throw," so give it to the Lord and tell Him that when He sees it is time to answer you, then it is up to Him to stir you to start seeking Him about the issue again. Trust Him to catch what you have thrown at Him, and believe He'll make the next move. That's a J.D. paraphrase of, "Commit your way to the Lord, trust also in Him, and He shall bring it to pass." The Revised Standard Version says "He will act." God will take the initiative and bring up the subject to you again when He sees the time is right and in your best interest to answer you. I have learned this lesson through many such experiences in my lifetime.

God's Ways and Purposes in Testing Us

Before we consider the many and varied ways God tests us, we need to understand that God is absolutely just and righteous. This means we can never blame Him, regardless of how puzzled we are by a delayed answer. "For the righteous God tests the hearts and minds" (Psalm 7:9).

1. A delay can be because God is testing us to see whether we're diligent seekers or casual inquirers. "For he who comes to God must believe that He is, and that He is a rewarder of those who diligently seek Him" (Hebrews 11:6).

Jeremiah 29:12–13 places importance on the singleness of purpose and intensity with which we seek God: "Then you will call upon Me and go and pray to Me, and I will listen to you. And you will seek Me and find Me, when you search for Me with all your heart."

Diligent seeking with persistence definitely gets God's attention. He encourages us not to give up from the parable Jesus told in Luke 18:1–8. The unjust judge finally granted the widow's request because she wouldn't take "no" for an answer. And the man finally got the bread he needed for his guests from his neighbor who was in bed at midnight because the man wouldn't quit knocking on his neighbor's door (see Luke 11:5).

However, my favorite verse to encourage persistency is found in Isaiah 21:12: "If you would ask, then ask; and come back yet again" (NIV). So much unanswered prayer is because we give up too soon.

2. God could be testing us as to whether we are going to rest in faith that He will answer us based on the knowledge of His character, and His promises that He will.

Are we really trusting in His faithfulness, knowing, believing, and declaring that He will not fail us? Are we feeding our faith by meditating on Deuteronomy 31:8? "And the LORD, He is the One who goes before you. He will be with you, He will not leave you nor forsake you; do not fear nor be dismayed." God actually hides Himself from us at times to test our faith—only because our faith will be stronger after it's tested by God's initial silence. "I will wait for the LORD, who is hiding His face from the house of Jacob, and I will hope in Him" (Isaiah 8:17 RSV).

3. The Lord may also be testing us when we have to give someone an answer related to a specific occasion or we have to give a message from the Lord, for instance, as a speaker at a meeting. Are we committed to seeking God until we hear from Him, and that we have nothing to say until He speaks? Now that's often a tough test. I know. I've had a bunch of them!

The surest way to pass these tests is to look at the life of the Lord Jesus when He was on earth. After all, He is our model and mentor. What did He do? From John 12:49–50 Jesus makes it clear that He never spoke anything other than what the Father told Him to say. And John 7:16–17 explains that when anyone speaks on his own authority he does so to bring honor to himself, not God. When God sends us to a person or situation, He may well test us in regard to what we are to say and when we are to say it.

I was teaching at a conference in Cyprus to a number of different missionary organizations that had come together from the Middle East. I had spoken in the morning and was scheduled to speak in the evening of the same day. I spent the afternoon seeking God for the message, but received nothing.

About 4.30 P.M. I asked the leader of the conference to join me in inquiring if God had another agenda. God strongly confirmed to us both from the Scriptures that I was to speak. I remained in my room seeking God.

The meeting started with worship at 7:00 P.M. and at 7:30 P.M. the leader announced that I would bring the word of the Lord. I still had no direction whatsoever, and explained that until I did, I had nothing to say.

Jesus was, and is, my mentor. He said, "For I have not spoken on My own authority; but the Father who sent Me gave Me a command, what I should say and what I should speak" (John 12:49). He also said, "He who speaks from himself seeks his own glory; but He who seeks the glory of the One who sent Him is true, and no unrighteousness is in Him" (John 7:18).

I continued seeking God. The leader asked the conferees to pray for the release of the message. They did. God was still silent. When you've chosen to be nothing so that He may become everything, you don't sweat it.

Exercising the rest of faith as taught in Hebrews chapters 3 and 4, I waited in silent expectancy. Forty minutes later, the Holy Spirit quickened two verses of Scripture to me related to waiting on God. Understanding came that I was not to give my teaching on that subject, but to share two stories out of my life of other severe testings and results from waiting on God for His agenda, in His timing, His way. I obeyed.

When the fear of the Lord is on us, we will choose His way every time. Through humility, faith, and obedience we'll experience that "the government will be upon His shoulder[s]" (Isaiah 9:6)—not ours.

4. God can also test us by delaying an answer to see whether we will understand the immense privilege of waiting on Him because of Who He is, or whether we will be impatient or resentful.

I had been seeking God on numerous occasions to know how to respond to an invitation to speak at a spiritual leadership conference, without receiving any answer. One day, the phone rang and the sponsors said they had to have my answer on that particular day in order to meet their publicity brochure deadline. I was desperate.

I had a full day of other ministry-related responsibilities planned. At 10:00 A.M. I knelt down by a chair in my bedroom and asked God to speak to me for the sake of the sponsors, and believed that in His faithfulness and infinite understanding He would come through. Five hours later, at 3:00 P.M., I was still there, having heard nothing.

I then said, "Thank You for the great privilege of waiting before Your blazing throne as You are seated there in Your dazzling beauty and magnificent splendor. Because of Who You are, impatience and resentment from me would be an insult to You. I will gladly continue to wait in Your majestic presence."

Very quietly but clearly, He then spoke one word into my spirit. "Yes." I had an answer. The test was passed because of the knowledge of God's character. This is where Psalm 69:13 and Micah 7:7, as quoted previously, are invaluable faith builders.

5. Another test may be whether or not we will receive God's answer through another person of proven ministry and character and let God confirm this answer to us. This is not

one of God's normal or usual methods, but He can be testing our humility by using it.

At the end of a whole day of seeking God for the word of the Lord at YWAM's University of the Nations campus in Kona, Hawaii, I had no understanding of the message for the evening meeting assignment. Many visitors were in attendance for that Friday night service. It came time for the start of the meeting. When I told my friend and leader, Loren Cunningham, my situation, the Holy Spirit directed him to say to me, "Preach the gospel." I immediately sensed this was my answer and said, "Thank you. I will." This experience had never happened to me before, nor has it happened since.

With zero time to prepare, the Holy Spirit came upon me and I preached the gospel based on the character of God without any notes. There was an unusual move of God among the people as I was directed to challenge them about making a first-time public commitment to Jesus as the Lord of their lives. This entailed their telling God that the answer would always be "yes" to anything He asked them to do, regardless of the cost. Fifteen people stood and verbally declared this first-time level of total commitment and abandonment to the Lordship of Jesus Christ. Praise His wonderful name. He is faithful.

6. God may be testing us to see if we are prepared to be given understanding from God when told to do something very difficult or unusual, knowing that the understanding may not come until after we've been obedient. Abraham is a classic example of this test. When God told him to go up Mount Moriah and sacrifice his son to God, he hadn't a clue how or when God would explain this extraordinarily difficult and perplexing command.

Only the fear of God and the knowledge of His character motivated Abraham to obey. He was severely tested but God came through not a minute too soon, or too late (see Genesis 22:11–12). God is always on time—His time! Jesus said to His disciple Peter, "What I am doing you do not understand now, but you will know after this" (John 13:7). The Lord Jesus is still saying that to us today from His living Word.

7. God's test for us could also be to see if we are prepared for the circumstances in our lives to get worse before God fulfills His promises to us. No matter how Joseph did it right, not only did it go wrong, but the circumstances became increasingly difficult to endure, let alone understand. From the devastating trauma of being abandoned in a pit as a teenager to being sold as a slave into a foreign country, from having his character assassinated and being horribly misjudged to being thrown in prison, it was hardly what we would call being given a break. It was the pits!

But God had not forgotten Joseph's address. In a momentous, monumental moment everything was reversed. God came through big-time and Joseph landed up with a permanent address at the Egyptian palace! Psalm 105:19 gives us understanding of this phenomenal saga. "Until the time that his word came to pass, the word of the LORD tested him."

8. Finally, and this is really the "jackpot" or the bottom line, from God's perspective: Are we prepared to wait until the maximum glory can be given to our precious Lord Jesus before He answers our prayers and fulfills His promises to us? Are we really living for His glory as the supreme desire of our hearts? If so, it will not matter how long we wait.

Section

5

Warnings and Explanations

Dealing with Deception
and Presumption

*W*e need to understand that satanic forces will strongly contest and oppose truth—especially a truth that brings us into closer friendship with God, making Him vividly real and personal. Experiencing God's detailed directions in our lives in any or all of the many ways He communicates with us certainly produces that. Therefore, we should not find it too surprising that we could experience some casualties along the way unless we heed the warnings.

Usually warnings apply mostly to the people who have yielded their wills completely to God, believe He's going to speak to them, and who start experiencing the thrill of having two-way conversations with the Almighty as a way of life.

Satanic forces are both strong and subtle in their attacks against those who have tapped the real thing by literally believing that God will fulfill the following promises:

> Lean on, trust in, and be confident in the Lord with all your heart and mind and do not rely on your own insight or understanding. In all your ways know, recognize, and acknowledge Him, and He will direct and make straight and plain your paths. (Proverbs 3:5–6 AMP)

> Thus says the LORD, your Redeemer, the Holy One of Israel: "I am the LORD your God, who teaches you to profit, who leads you by the way you should go." (Isaiah 48:17)

Satanic forces are angered and threatened by the transformation of life that inevitably comes from living the truths in this book. One method by which the devil and his demons attack is tempting us to become proud. If we've entertained thoughts of *I must be in a special category of Christians for God to speak to me like this, or as frequently,* or *I don't think many other Christians experience this kind of closeness to God,* we have already fallen prey to a lie and become proud.

The fact is that we are only one of multiplied millions of God's children to whom God communicates freely and frequently. Acts 17:26–28 describes how this way of life is God's normal standard for everyone:

> And He has made from one blood every nation of men to dwell on all the face of the earth, and has determined their appointed times and the boundaries of their dwellings, so that they should seek the Lord, in the hope that they might grope for Him and find Him, though He is not far from each one of us; for in Him we live and move and have our being . . . "For we are also His offspring."

Here again we see normal communication between parents and their children. We are all very ordinary people, so there are millions of others experiencing the same normal thing. The only difference among Christians worldwide is that some have allowed our extraordinary Lord Jesus to be more extraordinary through them than others. This comes through constant steps of humility, obedience, and faith toward God.

At this point we may realize that we have had some prideful thoughts. Isn't it a relief to know that the sure remedy for conviction of sin is to truly repent and receive God's forgiveness? Jesus said, "And you shall know the truth, and the truth shall make you free" (John 8:32).

Any undealt-with sin becomes a potential platform for the enemy to frequently attack us. And if we persistently sin in a given area in our lives, we can become bound in that area by satanic forces.

If we do not live lives of repentance, it is possible for people who started being led by the Holy Spirit to end up being led by deceiving spirits. Moreover, in Psalm 81:12 God says that those people who would not listen to and obey the voice of God as a way of life, He would finally "[give] them over to their own stubborn heart, to walk in their own counsels." Now that needs to be taken super-seriously.

I cannot imagine anything much worse than God's leaving me with the responsibility of making my own decisions in and for my life. I haven't the faintest idea what is the best thing for me. I've proved it hundreds of times. Only the One who created us knows how to fulfill us. Only the One who is omniscient knows all the factors associated with our choices. So many times we find out that what appeared to be the thing we would choose to do the least, when God was given the opportunity of making the decision and communicating it to us, turned out to be the very best thing that could have happened to us.

We do ourselves an enormous favor by listening to and obeying God's voice as a way of life. More than that, taking any other course of action is the height of folly.

How Can We Become Deceived?

God does not leave us to second-guess that question. "The pride of your heart has deceived you" (Obadiah 3).

Pride is thinking of ourselves in any other way than the way God knows us to be. I have observed over many years that, in every case where a person has become bound by a deceiving spirit, pride was the basis.

Fewer methods of Satan are more subtle than when he delegates a deceiving spirit to bring suggestions to our minds. Demons cannot read our thoughts, but they become aware of our pride through hearing things we say. Then they make suggestions to us that are a mixture of truth and error. That is the nature of deception. Satan tempted the Lord Jesus in the wilderness and said to Him, "If You are the Son of God, throw Yourself down" (from the pinnacle of the temple). He then said "For it is written: 'He shall give His angels charge over you' . . . and, 'In their hands they shall bear you up, lest you dash your foot against a stone'" (Luke 4:9–11). That was not the correct quotation from Psalm 91:11. The missing part in the middle was, "To keep You in all Your ways." Satan was tempting the Lord Jesus to act presumptuously apart from the Father's orders, and then insinuating that God would protect Him.

Many times I have heard people attribute certain quotations to the Bible, and when the statements were carefully checked, no such Biblical quotes were in the Bible. Often, people who know the Bible least will quote it incorrectly to support their own opinions.

Satanic forces can also influence our minds by twisting the meaning of Scriptures—even to the point of trying to convince us that we are to believe the exact opposite of the truth God has spoken in His Word. I know of instances in which that has happened, but the enemy's lies were exposed and the people set free.

We can always test these impressions by asking God the basic questions:

- Are they in line with what the Bible actually states?
- Do they match the overall teaching of God's Word on that subject?
- Are they in harmony with the character of God and the ways of God from the Word of God?

God will never tell us to do something that:

- is in any way unholy or harmful to another.
- is unloving.
- would lessen our love toward a life partner or a family member.
- hinders our witness for Christ.
- lessens our burden for lost souls.
- segregates us from the rest of the body of Christ by our choices.
- would bring dishonor to God's name.
- would give others a distorted view of God's character— although many times in the Bible God told His servants to do unusual things.

God will tell us to do things of which we have little or no understanding to test our level of the fear of the Lord and to test our basic trust in His character.

If we are not sure whether we have been deceived or not, as we seek God with all our heart He will reveal the truth to us about our condition. If we have become deceived and we sincerely want to be free, we follow through with the four action points below:

1. Humble ourselves before God, confess our pride, deeply repent before Him, and receive His forgiveness. "If we confess our sins, He is faithful and just to forgive us our sins and to cleanse us from all unrighteousness" (1 John 1:9).

2. We bind the deceiving spirit that has oppressed us in the name of the Lord Jesus Christ, and on the authority of God's Word, we loose ourselves from the evil spirit's grip, quoting the following Scriptures with faith in our hearts:

- "Assuredly, I say to you, whatever you bind on earth will be bound in heaven, and whatever you loose on earth will be loosed in heaven" (Matthew 18:18).

- "And you shall know the truth, and the truth shall make you free" (John 8:32).

- "Therefore if the Son makes you free, you shall be free indeed" (John 8:36).

- "He who is in you is greater than he who is in the world" (1 John 4:4).

3. Praise God for the victory Jesus won on the cross when He bowed His sacred head and said, "It is finished" (John

19:30). Praise Him for the power of His shed blood, by which the enemy is defeated. "And they overcame him by the blood of the Lamb and by the word of their testimony, and they did not love their lives to the death" (Revelation 12:11). Praise Him for His power over the enemy. "For this purpose the Son of God was manifested, that He might destroy the works of the devil" (1 John 3:8).

4. Heed the warning in Galatians 5:1: "Stand fast therefore in the liberty by which Christ has made us free, and do not be entangled again with a yoke of bondage."

Regardless of how long we have been in the bondage of deception or how deeply we have been entrenched in the sin of pride, we can take comfort and encouragement that, despite inevitable judgment from God, His mercy is always extended to a truly repentant heart. King Nebuchadnezzar is a classic example. After seven years of God's judgment as a result of persistent pride, through great humiliation, Nebuchadnezzar has this magnificent testimony of God's perfect character: "Now I, Nebuchadnezzar, praise and extol and honor the King of heaven, all of whose works are truth, and His ways justice. And those who walk in pride He is able to put down" (Daniel 4:37).

How to Avoid the Pitfalls of Deception

Because the sin of pride is our worst enemy (not the devil), we need to be frequently asking God to reveal by His Spirit any part of our heart where pride lurks. If not repented of, it will inevitably, in time, manifest itself to others: "For out of the abundance of the heart the mouth speaks" (Matthew 12:34).

Our pride is the sin to which we are the most blind. We can readily see it in others, but are so slow to recognize it in ourselves. That is pride's deceptive nature. That's why we need to frequently ask God to show us our hearts as only He sees them and believe that He will give us the needed revelation.

In Jeremiah 17:9 we read, "The heart is deceitful above all things, and desperately wicked; who can know it?" The answer to that question is found in 2 Chronicles 6:30: "Give to everyone according to all his ways, whose heart You know (for You alone know the hearts of the sons of men)." We are often blind to our impure motives, so we need to pray, "Make me know my transgression and my sin" (Job 13:23).

The following information is taken from an article I wrote on "The Release of the Spirit through Brokenness" in the *Women of Destiny Bible* (Copyright © 2000, Thomas Nelson, Inc. Used by permission).

Some of God's methods of answering these prayers are:

• Spiritual surgery with an instant answer, where the veil is lifted from our spiritual vision and we experience divine revelation and deep conviction of our pride and/or unbelief. "You have set our iniquities before You, our secret sins in the light of Your countenance" (Psalm 90:8).

• Spiritual surgery again, but where we have to wrestle with God with intense desire and persistent faith until He answers us, as He did Jacob (see Hosea 12:4).

• The drip-feed method—a gradual process whereby God allows circumstances in our lives that show, by our wrong reactions to them, what is in our hearts. Perhaps we responded ungraciously in a difficult situation, and the Holy Spirit reminds us that "God resists the proud, but gives grace to the humble" (James 4:6).

Making brokenness and repentance a way of life releases fresh revelation. "In Your light we see light" (Psalm 36:9), which means:

- We'll be given fresh revelation from God's Word.

- We will have light on the pathway of our life when we need directions from God.

- Understanding will be given to us by God in relation to perplexing situations—the causes and purposes of them.

The enemy's power to deceive us is defeated by our continuously choosing to walk in humility before God and other people. Satan's ways are based in pride, therefore we overcome him by having a broken and contrite spirit.

It is very important to quickly say to God and any others with whom we may have been seeking God for answers, "I'm sorry. I had a wrong impression," if what we thought was God's direction turned out to be something other than that. This act of openness and brokenness removes any platform from which the enemy can deceive us. It is also very important not to presume that we have had a wrong impression when that may not be true. I explain this further, later in this chapter.

Pride can be the motive if we are always wanting people to know when and how God speaks to us. We should check with the Holy Spirit before we share, when we share, and how much to share. This kind of wisdom is based in humility. "When pride comes, then comes shame; but with the humble is wisdom" (Proverbs 11:2 NKJV).

Timing is important. After Peter, James, and John had been on the Mount of Transfiguration, we read from Mark 9:9–10 that Jesus told them not to tell anyone what they had seen, until after Jesus' resurrection. Often, the greater revelation we receive from God, the more cautious we need to be about if or when we share it.

The apostle Paul received such profound revelation from God at one point in his life, that he was forbidden by Him to share any of it (see 2 Corinthians 12:4). In another instance, Queen Esther waited in the humility of wisdom for the right timing to declare her identity as a Jew in submission to Mordecai's direction (see Esther 4:14–16).

Another way to avoid the pitfalls of pride and possible subsequent deception is to immediately give God the glory in our minds whenever people remark about the ways and frequency by which we hear and know God's voice. We throw up a quick "telegram" response to God, and then if possible a verbal response to people, such as, "It's all by God's grace alone. We take no credit."

We must also guard against any unwillingness to gladly receive the voice of the Lord through others with proven characters and ministries, whether in regard to revelation of truth, exhortation, or rebuke.

Perhaps the safest way to guard against deception is to have a true spirit of submission to those over us in authority. "Likewise you younger people, submit yourselves to your elders.

Yes, all of you be submissive to one another, and be clothed with humility, for 'God resists the proud, but gives grace to the humble'" (1 Peter 5:5).

Having an independent spirit makes us extremely vulnerable to satanic suggestions. Whereas, having a submissive spirit to God's appointed leaders, puts us in a place of protection. "Remember those who rule over you, who have spoken the word of God to you, whose faith follow, considering the outcome of their conduct" (Hebrews 13:7). Leaders need to be operating in the fear of the Lord and be submissive to other leadership to earn the right to be trusted.

How Can We Know If We've Been Led by Deceiving Spirits?

We must clearly understand that all lack of fulfillment in relation to following impressions we believe came from God, does not automatically mean that they did not originate with Him. God could have been testing us to see whether we would obey Him, as He did with Abraham (see Genesis 22:9–12).

We may also have been presumptuous in our interpretation of a certain direction, and interposed our human ideas without pressing in to God for clear understanding from Him. And remember the other reasons God delays answers in Chapter 7 of this book.

However, the lack of fulfillment in following impressions we thought were from God can be the activity of deceiving spirits upon our minds and spirits. We need to understand that Satan's tactics are to try to get us to listen to his suggestions, while trying to convince us they came from God. And then, when there is no fulfillment because Satan is a liar, he tries to convince us that God can't be trusted, in the hope that we'll lose faith in Him. The implications are horrendous, unless *we're thoroughly grounded in and have true revelation of the character of God.*

If we don't, we will be tempted to throw our Christian faith overboard, or go through the motions of being a Christian who loves and trusts God on the outside, but inwardly resents Him, does not trust Him to guide, is skeptical and cynical of people who do, and ceases to seek God at a personal level. Those people are really saying by their attitude toward God, "I did what You said, but You have not done what You said You would do."

Early in our married life, Jim and I were friends with two other young married couples, the husbands of which were particularly zealous Christians. One evening, both young men received the impression that they were to drive out to our home to visit us. We were not at home that evening, so they sat in one of their cars for hours outside our house waiting, until it became too late to continue.

Their "guidance" did not work out, and to our utter dismay and disappointment we heard they had given up their Christian faith. That was the reaction of pride and unbelief. All they had to do was to ask God to show them what He wanted to teach them, press in to Him, and guard against presumption until He gave full understanding.

When we are convinced that God is utterly righteous, true and faithful in circumstances like I've described, we should simply say, "I do not understand the outcome of what I thought were steps of obedience I've taken to You, God. But because Your character is flawless and You are faithful, I believe

You will give me understanding in Your way and time." That is the response of humility and faith.

Our greatest need is the knowledge of the character of God. When we have that, we go on to say to Him, "Obviously, in Your infinite knowledge and wisdom and unfathomable love for me, You have things to teach me. There must be purposes for my good in these puzzling circumstances, and because of Your justice, as I seek You with all my heart, You will show me what they are."

God responds to this humility and faith by reminding us that "He is the Rock, His work is perfect; for all His ways are justice, a God of truth and without injustice; righteous and upright is He" (Deuteronomy 32:4). We also know that "He is a rewarder of those who diligently seek Him" (Hebrews 11:6).

Some Further Explanations

Don't be discouraged or alarmed if you get impressions that you don't understand or are obviously wrong. Just thank God that, in His faithfulness, He will enable you to learn how to know when He is speaking and what He is saying as you grow in the knowledge of Him. A dear minister friend of mine, who heard this teaching on divine guidance for the first time, experienced hearing God's voice with detailed accuracy and was really excited. God answered his personal question by naming the exact Bible book, chapter, and verse. He had no idea what to expect, but it proved to be right on. This was a brand-new experience for him.

The next time he asked God a question related to his church, he received the impression of a Bible book, chapter, and verse, and it had nothing to do with the needed answer. Because he is a mature man of God he didn't reject the first answer or question God's method of speaking. He simply said, "That's okay, God. You are obviously showing me that it was Your voice the first time and my voice the second time. I was not as dead to my own thoughts as I should have been."

If two or more people are seeking God for answers, and receive different impressions, go back to God again and ask Him what it is He is trying to say. Keep seeking Him until the understanding comes.

At the close of a powerful time of intercession I was having with three students in a YWAM training school, I asked them to seek God with me to see if He had anything more to say. Immediately, I opened my Bible to a portion of Scripture with understanding that we were to present Him with a major-sized request. When I asked the other three to share what they had received, all three said they did not get anything that made sense. When I pressed for specifics, each one had been given, with differing methods as described in this book, the exact Scriptures God had given me.

Later, in the classroom, when this was being shared, another student had been directed to the same portion without having any understanding. Because all four of those students were unfamiliar with the understanding of that portion of Scripture, they had thrown out the guidance God was wanting to give us as a school, related to a major prayer request. Don't hold back from sharing an impression simply because you have no understanding about it. Others in the group may have understanding. Also, if you are asking God if you are to do something or go somewhere, and some get "Yes," and some get "No," it could be "Yes," but not in the timing in which you had presumed.

Again, don't presume you have had a wrong impression if at first things do not appear to be working out. Go back to God again, ask Him for confirmation or correction and then obey whatever He reveals, regardless of the circumstances.

My husband, Jim, our son, John, and I were going to a YWAM staff conference in Switzerland. After seeking God, He had spoken, naming a specific date we were to depart from California. When we went to book the tickets, the agent said there were no seats available on any airlines on that date, so we booked them for another day. This disturbed me, so we went back and insisted that we had to leave on the date we had originally requested. God honored the obedience to follow His detailed instructions. We ended up being rerouted and all three put in the front-row seats of first class, where Jim had the opportunity of witnessing to a non-Christian businessman during the long flight. We only paid for coach class tickets!

Also, we must remember that God gave Jonah a clear message to give to the city of Ninevah. After initially disobeying God, he finally delivered it. Because of the depth of the people's repentance of sin, God changed His mind and the outcome was the opposite of what the message predicted. But that did not mean Jonah's message was false (see Jonah, chapters 1–4).

God told Moses He was going to annihilate the children of Israel. The message was clear. Through Moses' intercession, God changed His mind. The outcome was the exact opposite, but that did not mean God's original message to Moses was false (see Exodus 32:9–14).

God's promises are so often conditional. They go like this:

"If you will, I will." God had promised the children of Israel that He would take them into Caanan, but because they did not fulfill the conditions, He reversed the promise. All but Joshua and Caleb and the younger generation under twenty years old died and never made it. Moses, Joshua, Caleb, or the elders did not have a wrong impression. How we need to check our lives in God's presence and see whether the sins of unbelief, murmuring, fearfulness, and disobedience are hindering God from fulfilling His promises to us and, therefore, our destinies.

Treat pride and unbelief like the plague. The Bible says, "He leads the humble in what is right, and teaches the humble his way" (Psalm 25:9 RSV).

Here's a final important point which can help us not to make unrighteous judgments against others or even ourselves. God can have spoken clearly to us in relation to His purposes for another person. Following that, in any time frame, the person or people closely connected with that person can make choices, whether verbalized or not, that could cause God to change His mind. That is part of God's sovereignty and people's free will. So, what God originally told us may not come to pass. In those instances it would not mean that what we received was necessarily false. No wonder God says to "judge nothing before the time, until the Lord comes, . . . and reveal[s] the counsels of the hearts. Then each one's praise will come from God" (1 Corinthians 4:5).

A friend of mine was suffering greatly and was terminally ill. I diligently sought God to speak to me from His Word if He intended to bring healing. From the clarity of the specific Scriptures given me through several different methods by which God chose to speak, His answer was a resounding "yes."

When the person died, I was shocked and perplexed to say the least. I was desperate for God's explanation. I will never forget His answer, spoken clearly into my spirit. "I spoke to you and you obeyed by declaring what I had given you. But you don't know what transpired between your friend and Me after I had spoken to you."

Those words brought great enlightenment and relief. We're never enlightened or surprised by what comes from our own thoughts. But when God speaks there's always an element of wonderment and awe.

This experience helped me never to quickly come to conclusions about the final outcome of my earnest inquiries and sincere steps of obedience and faith to God on behalf of others.

Section

6

The Importance, Characteristics of
Bible Standards, and Evidences
of Obedience

The Evidences, Consequences, and
Checklists Related to Disobedience

The only purpose in your reading everything in this book to this point is to make it easier for you to appropriate the truths in this section. We discern God's voice more clearly for these reasons—that we may more fully obey Him, which in turn causes us to more thoroughly know Him, so that we are able to more accurately make Him known.

Unconditional obedience to God should be our love response to Him for His unconditional love to us. This removes all the dutiful dullness from our responses to His directions. Every influence God brings into our lives to encourage us to obey Him is so that we will do so because of *who He is.*

So what is He really like? He is:

- Supreme in His authority
- Dazzling in His beauty
- Flawless in His character
- Ingenious in His creativity
- Timeless in His existence
- The most exciting Person
- Unswerving in His faithfulness
- Matchless in His grace

- Blazing in His glory

- Unparalleled in His greatness

- Awesome in His holiness

- Incomprehensible in His humility

- The Author of humor

- The ultimate in intensity

- Absolute in His justice

- Infinite in His knowledge and wisdom

- Unfathomable in His love

- The Fountain of life

- Unending in His mercy

- The Owner of everything

- Limitless in His power

- Fascinating in His personality

- Majestic in His splendor

- Indescribable in His tenderness

- Unquestionable in His sovereignty

- The personification of truth

- Unsearchable in His understanding

- Terrible in His wrath

- Mysterious in His ways

- The Ruler of an eternal, indestructible kingdom

- The reigning Monarch of the universe

- King God

- The Lover of my soul

He is the One who has totally captivated me, and the only One who can totally fulfill me.

In the light of that description, can you see that we do ourselves the greatest favor by running to obey Him?

When we all stand at the judgment seat and give an account of our lives to God, and see Him as He really is, we will find it unthinkable that we even entertained the thought of disobedience to Him for one moment. We will look into His eyes, blazing with the fire of unfathomable love for us and with the fire of His white-hot holiness.

Because of who God is, it is not only the height of preposterous pride to disobey Him, it is totally illogical. Because the Bible tells us that obedience to God is always for our good and our children's good. "Oh, that they had such a heart in them that they would fear Me and always keep all My commandments, that it might be well with them and with their children forever!" (Deuteronomy 5:29).

More than that, God promises us repeatedly in Deuteronomy chapter 11 and chapter 28, and Leviticus chapter 26, that if we will obey Him, He will bless us; and that if we disobey Him, He will punish us. God keeps all of His promises. Disobeying Him is the same as telling Him to hold back all of the blessings that come with obedience, and bring on all the punishments that come with disobedience. That is not only stupidity, it's insanity.

In the first fourteen verses of Deuteronomy 28, God tells

us that He will bless us when we obey Him. But then He takes fifty-three verses to tell us that He will bring judgment on our disobediences. Why are the negative consequences related to disobedience given at a ratio of almost four to one? Because God knows the tendencies of the human heart. We will readily believe the rewards of obedience, but we do not want to believe the punishments of disobedience because we have a warped view of God's character. His disciplines are always for our good, to keep us from harm, and to bless us; not to deprive us.

There was a time in my life when I lay on my face on the floor and read through Deuteronomy 11, Deuteronomy 28, and Leviticus 26, slowly meditating on the solemnity of the subject of obedience, and did not get up from the floor until I totally believed what God said. It was a life-changing experience. It brought the character of God into clear focus. It balanced the love and mercy of God with the fear of the Lord, the holiness of God, and the judgment of God. Deuteronomy 28:58 says that the purpose of understanding the consequences of disobedience to God's voice is "that you may fear this glorious and awesome name, THE LORD YOUR GOD." In Jeremiah 5:4 God says, "They do not know the way of the LORD, the judgment of their God."

When God punishes us for disobedience, He does so with the strong hope that the punishment will be used to keep us from further disobedience. That is an act of genuine love, not revenge. Unconditional obedience is the key to a successful Christian life. Think about that!

In 1 Peter 1:2 we read that we are "chosen and destined

by God the Father and sanctified by the Spirit for obedience to Jesus Christ" (RSV). That means that obedience to Him is where all the action and fulfillment is.

Therefore, the basis of all frustration and lack of fulfillment lies in disobedience to revealed truth, the truths in God's Word, and the promptings of the Holy Spirit. Many times it's not more truth that we need; it's more obedience to already revealed truth. "Therefore, to him who knows to do good and does not do it, to him it is sin" (James 4:17). This verse defines "sins of commission." Many times the "sins of omission" are the ones to which we are blind or insensitive, but for which we will be equally accountable to God as we will be for the sins of commission.

Can you imagine how it disappoints and hurts the heart of God when He has planned to bless us in ways beyond our imagination, and then we choose not to take some simple step of obedience because with our little finite minds, we cannot understand why God has to withhold all those benefits? This scenario is being repeated all too frequently. The more implications involved with large steps of obedience and faith to God, the more glory will be brought to the Lord Jesus, the more His Kingdom will be extended, and the greater blessings will be ultimately showered upon us. We seldom see those blessings immediately.

As I have previously mentioned, in 1971 God called us to leave our home in New Zealand to become missionaries with YWAM. This meant living entirely by faith with two teenage children. We had very little money and not one person guaranteed us one penny of support, although our friends and church believed in our call from God. We were totally "out on a limb," with nothing but God's call, God's character, and God's promises. That's when we chose to tell God, that for the rest of our lives, every bit of money He would give us would belong to Him, and that we would give any amount, any time, to anyone He indicated. We went from tithing 10 percent to giving Him the right to have it all. Thirty years later, at the time of writing this book, we can say that consistently living at that radical level of commitment and faith, by His grace, we have been greatly blessed.

Of course there have been numerous times of severe testings when God required us to give everything, when we were in desperate need ourselves. But that is God's way of strengthening and increasing our faith. God has never failed us, simply because He cannot fail. Faithfulness is part of His character. But I know for certain that obedience to Him because of who He is, is the key to this level of obedience and faith.

We desperately need to take the time to study God's character, facet by facet, in order to know Him. "But the people who know their God shall be strong, and carry out great exploits" (Daniel 11:32).

God promises us His joy and peace when we obey the Great Commission that Jesus gave to all His disciples in Matthew 28:18–20. "For you shall go out with joy, and be led out with peace" (Isaiah 55:12). That is our testimony as a missionary family.

God's peace always accompanies obedience to Him. And isn't peace of mind what we are all seeking?

Now is the time to look into the Biblical standard of obedience. It has three characteristics.

1. Instant Obedience

David said, "I made haste, and did not delay to keep Your commandments" (Psalm 119:60). God makes it clear that we are not to delay when He tells us to give money or possessions to others. "Do not withhold good from those to whom it is due, when it is in the power of your hand to do so. Do not say to your neighbor 'Go and come back, and tomorrow I will give it,' when you have it with you" (Proverbs 3:27–28).

I learned this lesson when I was seeking understanding as to what I was to speak before addressing a meeting. When I could get no answer, I asked God if there was any undealt-with sin in my life that was causing the silence. Immediately He reminded me of the monetary gifts He had told us to give to two different missionaries, and because of the busyness of our lives, we had delayed in writing the notes and mailing the checks. Only when that was taken care of did I hear God's voice directing me to the message I was to prepare. That was a vivid lesson in learning that delayed obedience is disobedience.

2. Whole Obedience

Saul kept back some of the sheep and oxen when God had told him to destroy everything in relation to the Amalekites (see 1 Samuel 15:18–23). This partial obedience cost Saul the loss of the anointing of the Holy Spirit and in time his leadership position. Ananias and Sapphira lied, and kept back part of the money that was to have been given to God from the sale of their property. It cost them their lives (see Acts 5:1–11). They learned the hardest way that partial obedience is disobedience. We need to heed the powerful warning from their lack of the fear of the Lord.

3. Joyful Obedience

The children of Israel were in the will of God by being in the wilderness. But they frequently murmured and complained. We can be *positionally obedient* by being in the right place at the right time, but *conditionally disobedient* because we're not delighting ourselves in the Lord and delighting to do His will.

In Deuteronomy 28:45, 47 God states that His judgments will come upon those of you who "did not obey the voice of the LORD your God, to keep His commandments and statutes which He commanded you . . . because you did not serve the LORD your God with joy and gladness of heart, for the abundance of everything."

The children of Israel learned that obedience with murmuring is disobedience. Coupled with unbelief and rebellion, it cost them the fulfillment of their destinies—all but Caleb and Joshua.

We can say by our own disobedient lives that the price of obeying God is too high. The truth is, the price of disobedience is higher. We may think that God's disciplines are too great. The fact is that they prove to be beneficial in every way.

We may have decided that the standard of the Word of God is unattainable and impractical. The truth is that God's grace and the Holy Spirit's enablement are available for every step of obedience to God. And when we act upon God's Word by applying it to our lives, we are set free (see John 8:32).

An associate pastor once told me that disobedience to God's directions to pursue five months of YWAM's training resulted in the following:

- The anointing of the Holy Spirit lifted off his preaching ministry.

- The vision for reaching the nations with the gospel faded.

- He was unable to hear God's voice for directions.

- A general spiritual dullness settled upon him, making him insensitive to the promptings of the Holy Spirit.

What a horrendous price to pay for disobedience. That's the bad news. The good news is that the same pastor repented, took a three-month YWAM "Crossroads" course, plus a two-month overseas outreach, and retrieved all he had forfeited. What a merciful, longsuffering God!

We Are the Only Ones Who Can Thwart God's Will for Our Lives

While disobedience to God thwarts the fulfillment of God's plans and purposes for our lives, obedience to God releases them—in time, every time. Because *God always makes a way for those who believe and obey.*

Some of you may be thinking, *Do you mean to tell me that no one else and no circumstances can stop what God has planned for me?* Oh yes I do, on the authority of God's Word. Listen to what He says: "I will cry to God Most High, to God who performs *all things* for me. He shall send from heaven and save me;

He reproaches the one who would swallow me up. God shall send forth His mercy and His truth" (Psalm 57:2–3).

Now, grasp the certainty of these statements.

- "But He is unique, and who can make Him change? And *whatever* His soul desires, *that He does.* For He performs what is appointed for me, and many such things are with Him" (Job 23:13–14).

- "I know that You can do *everything,* and that no purpose of Yours can be withheld from You" (Job 42:2).

Keep tracking with me. It gets even better.

- "Surely, as I have thought, so it shall come to pass, and as I have purposed, so it shall stand" (Isaiah 14:24).

- "For the LORD of hosts has purposed, and who will annul it? His hand is stretched out, and who will turn it back?" (Isaiah 14:27).

Perhaps you're thinking, *Well tell me how this works in everyday situations.* I'd be delighted.

I had been teaching all week at a conference in Seoul, Korea. An eighteen-year-old university student had heard me teach on the fear of the Lord, and about how God will always make a way for those who believe and obey. He believed what I taught from God's Word, and then God tested him.

YWAM was having a three-month course in discipleship training for Koreans in New York. God told the young Korean that he was to attend. This meant getting a passport. He was aware that at that time in Korea it was against the law for anyone who was a student, or who had not done military training, to obtain a passport.

Undaunted, the student obeyed God and went and filled out the application forms. When the official looked at him and the forms, he asked if the student was aware of the restrictions as mentioned above. The student said he was very aware of them and declared he was a student and had not done military training.

The somewhat-irritated official asked the obvious question. "Then why on earth are you making this application at this time?" With quiet authority the young Korean Christian simply said, "Because I fear God, and He told me to go to New York for missionary training." The stunned official then said the unheard of: "Then in that case, I'll grant you a passport," and proceeded with the processing of it.

You see, God's Word works. What is impossible to man is easy street for God. The "adventure" part of what I'm teaching in this book only happens when we *obey* God's voice. And believe me, it's some adventure—the greatest adventure known to mankind—the most challenging, most exciting, the most rewarding, and the most fulfilling.

The Importance of Obedience in Small Things

Obedience to God is important and rewarding regardless of the circumstances. In other words, God is not more impressed by our steps of obedience to do something that might seem more spectacular than when we obey Him in some little, obscure way.

It was just as important to God and to the Lord Jesus when Jesus took a little child in His arms and blessed him in obedience to the Father's orders as when He raised Lazarus from the dead.

We will never know the fulfillment of the revealed or unrevealed or partially revealed future until we become obedient in the things of the present. God never opens a big door of opportunity in Christian ministry to make Him known until we have been consistently obedient in numerous little things. This is the key that unlocks the doors whereby God is able to trust us with greater responsibilities and privileges in His Kingdom. "He who is faithful in what is least is faithful also in much" (Luke 16:10).

Many times the biggest opportunities to make God known come to us immediately after obeying Him in some small circumstance where we have no clue whatsoever as to the outcome, or even why it was important—other than because God spoke. That is the story of my entire life. When we make listening to God's voice a way of life in the little circumstances, we will be far more readily able to hear His voice in times of crisis when our survival can literally depend on it. Proverbs 1:33 says: "But whoever listens to me will dwell safely, and will be secure, without fear of evil."

In 1933, Peter Iliyn's father was five years old and was part of a number of Christian families who secretly left Communist Russia because of severe famine. They were miraculously protected and guided by the Holy Spirit into China.

For security reasons, they walked during the night and rested among the bushes during the day. On one occasion they relied on their own judgment and disobeyed the directions of the Holy Spirit. This resulted in their finding themselves without any food or water. They searched unsuccessfully for water all night one night, and by the time the sun was hot the next day, they were desperate. The babies and children were particularly distraught. They all cried out to God in anguish, "Father, give us water or we'll die." In His mercy, God answered by speaking prophetically through a member of the group. "Children, turn left. Walk a short distance and I will give you water."

As they obeyed, the men noticed bulrushes ahead, which indicated water. They dug down through the sand. First, murky water emerged, but the farther they dug, the clearer it became. They drank and drank and rested that day until they had enough strength to walk again that night.

The entire dangerous journey was marked by the group's following the specific directions given by several members through the operation of the gifts of the Holy Spirit as described in 1 Corinthians 14.

Disobedience to God in the small things can at times almost cost us our lives. This was illustrated in the last story, and because of the importance of understanding this truth, I'm going to tell you another story I heard on a Christian TV network which vividly underscores it.

One afternoon a Christian young woman planned to take her baby and drive over to a friend's house. When she was ready to leave her house she heard a clear voice speaking into her spirit saying, "Stay at home." That didn't fit into her plans so she ignored it and walked out to her car. She had just finished placing her child in the baby seat in the backseat of the car, when two strange men suddenly confronted her. At gunpoint, they ordered her into the backseat and drove off.

Despite all her pleadings and questions, they refused to give her any understanding as to the purpose of the abduction and kidnapping, or any clue as to their destination.

The next hour was a horror story of mental torment. Amazingly she somehow managed to speak to her husband at his workplace by using her cell phone. And she verbally called on the name of the Lord for divine intervention. After a series of miracles, the police finally located her on a freeway and released her from a horrendous experience.

What a price to pay for the sin of disobedience to the promptings of the Holy Spirit! How we desperately need to take God seriously and to submit our wills to His will. It could make the difference between life and death.

God's warnings to the children of Israel in Deuteronomy 30:19–20 are as pungent, pertinent, and predictable as tomorrow morning's sunrise. Let's ponder them seriously, to the point of acting upon them as a way of life.

> I call heaven and earth as witnesses today against you, that I have set before you life and death, blessing and cursing; therefore choose life, that both you and your descendants may live; that you may love the LORD your God, that you may obey His voice, and that you may cling to Him, for He is your life and the length of your days. (Deuteronomy 30:19–20)

The Link Between Love and Obedience

You will notice that in Deuteronomy 30:19–20 (see above), God links loving Him with obeying Him. Jesus said "If you love Me, keep My commandments" (John 14:15). I was once counseling a dear Christian woman who told me that she loved the Lord with all her heart and that He had been so good to her over the years, but she found it difficult to have time in the Bible on a daily basis. This was an area of neglect in her life.

My response was that before I could give her the practical help she needed, she would have to get honest with God. She needed to confess her lack of love to Him because of her disobedience to revealed truth. While this came as a shock to her, she realized the truth of it in the light of John 14:15, in which Jesus says: "If you love Me, keep My commandments."

That day she wept and deeply repented before God for her lack of love to Him. Since then, she has written and told me what a life-changing experience that was, because obedience to God is now viewed as it should be—an act from an overflow of love to Him. She also testified that her love for God had greatly increased since disciplining her life to make time for God in His Word, inviting the Holy Spirit to reveal God's character and ways to her, and seeking His face for Himself, not just His hand in provision, as I had counseled her.

I had told her to think about the Bible as God's love letter to her and to approach it with an excited anticipation of wondering what the Lover of her soul would have to say to her each day. This concept totally transformed her thinking from one of a dutiful approach to God to an intimate exchange of hearing her Lover's voice, and her responding back in praise and worship, all through reading the Word of God. Bible reading became a delight.

Obeying Others While Disobeying God

In Exodus 4:24–26 we read about the time in Moses' life when he listened to his wife Zipporah's preferences, at the expense of obeying God's orders. It almost cost him his life.

God had commissioned Moses to lead the children of Israel out of Egypt into Canaan. En route to that mind-boggling assignment, we read these startling words: "The LORD met Him and sought to kill him" (Exodus 4:24).

This is the classic incident in the Word of God to prove to us that no one is indispensable to God. He simply was not interested in having a disobedient leader on His hands.

Moses knew very well that every Jewish boy was to be circumcised on the eighth day, but he had not followed through in obedience.

God already knew that He would bring judgment on the Egyptian sons, their firstborn, and God had just told Moses that very thing (see Exodus 4:23). How could God do that when His ambassador to the Egyptians was living in disobedience to God in relation to his firstborn son? He couldn't. God is a God of justice.

So why did Zipporah immediately jump into action with a sharp stone and perform the necessary surgery on her baby boy? Because she saw God's reaction to Moses' procrastination and knew that his delayed obedience was disobedience, which would result in either a bloody baby or a dead husband.

Twice, Zipporah displayed her obvious disapproval and distaste for the Jewish law of circumcision by stating to Moses "You are a husband of blood" (v. 26). This strongly suggests to me that she had been influencing Moses to at least delay the painful procedure, probably hoping that, in time, he would decide that this Jewish custom was not that important. Remember, she was not a Hebrew, but a Midianite.

So why didn't God attempt to kill Zipporah? Because Moses was the head of his home and the God-appointed leader of a nation. Therefore, he was the one most accountable to God.

Moses was the only one who could thwart the accomplishment of God's will in his life, regardless of his wife's negative influences. Each of us is ultimately responsible and accountable to God for the choices we make in relation to revealed truth. We cannot blame satanic forces for tempting us or other people's negative pressures.

Saul disobeyed the voice of God and obeyed the voice of the people because he feared their reactions, and Samuel's cryptic comment was, "You have rejected the word of the LORD, and the LORD has rejected you from being king over Israel" (1 Samuel 15:26).

In 1 Kings 13, we read about a man of God who had been spectacularly used of God in the house of God one day. God had given him implicit instructions not to eat bread or drink water, or to return home by the way that he came. Then an older prophet lied and told him that an angel had appeared to him and said, by the word of the Lord, that the young man of God could go to the older prophet's house and eat bread and drink water. The younger man disobeyed God and obeyed the older prophet. The tragic result of the younger man's disobedience was death (see v. 24).

Again we see that God is not impressed by how mightily we have been used by Him in the past if we are presently living in disobedience. This is another example of the fact that no one is indispensable to God.

Disobeying God When He Speaks to Us
Through Another Person

In 2 Chronicles 35:21–22, we read about the time King Josiah rejected the word of the Lord when given a warning by Necho, king of Egypt, to refrain from going to war with him, lest Josiah be destroyed. The Bible says in verse 22, "Josiah . . . did not heed the words of Necho from the mouth of God . . ." The result was death. This is the story of a righteous young man being raised up by God to lead a nation in reformation, restoration, and renewal in remarkable ways, and yet through pride and presumption, he disobeyed a warning from God through someone God had sent to him. With God, it's how we finish that counts.

In 1 Chronicles 21, we read about King David's ordering Joab to number the people of Israel when God had not given the order to do so. Despite Joab's strong warning against this act of presumption, through pride, David resisted Joab and used his position of authority to force the orders to be carried out. This action resulted in the heaviest judgment David experienced from God in his entire life.

God had told Moses to number the Israelites in Numbers 1:1–3, so there is nothing intrinsically wrong with numbering the people at God's command. God is always absolutely just and righteous in His judgments (see Deuteronomy 32:4). He also knows the motives of the heart, by which we will ultimately be judged (see Romans 2:16; 1 Corinthians 4:5).

If David numbered Israel because he was relying on numerical strength instead of the power of God during that time in his leadership, or if he did it out of any other impure motive, that would have added to the severity of God's judgment (see Jeremiah 17:10).

Evidences of Disobedience to God

1. Disobedience to God is evidence of the lack of knowledge of who God is. (Refer back to the description of God in Chapter 1.) "Now by this we know that we know Him, if we keep His commandments. He who says, 'I know Him,' and does not keep His commandments, is a liar, and the truth is not in him" (1 John 2:3–4).

2. Disobedience to God is evidence that we do not take time in His presence for the purpose of knowing Him. Sadly, it seems that the body of Christ knows relatively nothing about trembling in the presence of the One who causes mountains to quake and melt like wax and the earth to heave at His presence.

Every time we read the Bible, we would be wise to ask God to reveal more of His character and ways to us, and believe that He will. He will also reveal Himself to us through unhurried times of worship and taking time to intercede for others. The more revelation we have of God's character, the more incentive we should have to obey Him. "Bless the LORD, you His angels, who excel in strength, who do His word" (Psalm 103:20).

Because Lucifer had great revelation of God, but chose to rebel and disobey Him, we understand the awesome responsibility of mankind's free will. Pride avoids God's presence and rebels. Humility yearns for God's presence and obeys.

3. Disobedience to God is a sign of pride. It means that we place more importance on our assessment of a given situation than God's. Imagine the audacity of mere, finite mortals, created from dust, concluding that we have better judgment than the One who is timeless in His existence and infinite in knowledge and wisdom. Pride is appalling.

4. Disobedience to God is a sign of unbelief in God's ability to work in a given situation when we cannot find a solution or understand His strategy. A classic example of this truth is found in the way Moses argued with God when He called Moses into leadership, as seen throughout Exodus 3–7. Only when Moses started to hearken to God's voice in obedience do we read that God hearkened unto Moses' voice when he petitioned God in difficult circumstances. So much unanswered prayer is the result of disobedience.

Evidences of Unconditional Obedience to God

1. Unconditional obedience to God is first the evidence that above all else we desire intimate friendship with God. "You are My friends if you do whatever I command you" (John 15:14).

This means that we take seriously everything He says to us. It means that it is of paramount importance to us to live with the knowledge of God's approval and to experience the joy and peace that accompany it.

As the Father loved Me, I also have loved you; abide in My love. If you keep My commandments, you will abide in My love, just as I have kept My Father's commandments and abide in His love. These things I have spoken to you, that

My joy may remain in you, and that your joy may be full. This is My commandment, that you love one another as I have loved you. (John 15:9–12)

This means that we are only as close to God as we allow His unconditional love to flow through us to all others. So what level of intimacy are we experiencing with the Lord Jesus? How important is it to us that God's peace reigns in our hearts at all times? I will illustrate from an adaptation of a story taken from *By Guess Or By God,* by Neville Winger.

One morning, while a seventy-year-old woman in New Zealand was having her daily Bible reading, she was arrested by a Scripture that spoke about going to a mountain and waiting. She seriously pondered the verse, but received no understanding so went on reading. Immediately she felt the departure of the peace of God. Because she knew that peace was a sign of the Holy Spirit's presence, she went back and read the verse again. The peace instantly returned, assuring her that God had spoken.

The lady asked God what He was trying to say. "Which mountain?" Immediately the mountain of Te Aroha was impressed upon her spirit. This mountain was about thirty miles from her home. She walked to the nearest town and caught a bus to the town of Te Aroha, often wondering if she was doing something foolish. When she looked up at the high mountain she said, "What now Lord?" The answer came back, "Start climbing."

This obedient elderly woman slowly plodded up the mountain trail. After about thirty minutes she came to a look-out spur. To her relief she noticed a wooden seat. On it was seated a young man. As she approached him, she had a deep sense of the Lord's presence, and an understanding that this was the purpose of her unusual mission.

The young man looked to be in bad shape, so she came right to the point. "Young man, God has sent me nearly thirty miles to talk to you. It must be important. What's the matter?" After a brief, stunned silence, he burst into tears and told her that he had climbed the mountain track to attempt suicide. He said he didn't have the courage to jump into a river and drown, and that every time he tried to tip his car over, he couldn't do it. He explained that in desperation, he had come up the mountain looking for somewhere to jump off, but the track only led to the lookout.

Without delay, the woman shared with him the wonderful news of God's redeeming love through the person of the Lord Jesus Christ's death and resurrection, and that He was the answer to every human need.

The young man received the Lord Jesus Christ by faith, as his personal Savior and committed his whole life to Him. The young man's new life in Christ started with assisting the lady down the mountain and driving her back to her home.

2. Obedience is also the evidence of the degree of love that we have for God. "This is love for God: to obey His commands. And His commands are not burdensome" (1 John 5:3 NIV).

3. The degree of the fear of the Lord upon us will determine the degree of obedience to God in our lives.

When Abraham passed the ultimate test of unconditional obedience to God by preparing to slay his son Isaac, it is significant what the angel of the Lord said after he restrained him from doing that act. "Now I know that you fear God, since you have not withheld your son, your only son, from Me" (Genesis 22:12).

The fear of the Lord means being more impressed with God's reactions to our actions than with other people's reactions. Proverbs 8:13 says, "The fear of the LORD is to hate evil." Abraham hated the sin of disobedience to God more than he loved his son Isaac. He was so convinced of God's faithfulness that he believed God would raise Isaac from the dead in order for God to fulfill His promises to Abraham.

The fear of the Lord and the knowledge of God's character will be the only things during times of severe testing that will motivate us to follow through with God's instructions when we may have to obey God without having any understanding why. I have been in that situation many times.

Once when I was speaking at a spiritual leadership conference in Chattanooga, Tennessee, I had given the first three points of my message entitled "The Fear of the Lord," having spoken for about twenty minutes. I had just finished saying that when the fear of the Lord is upon us we will always obey God, regardless of how unusual, perplexing or difficult the circumstances.

Instantly, the Holy Spirit spoke into my spirit, "Sit down and don't say another word." I simply told the audience what God had spoken, and without any other comments sat down. The chairman of the conference took over and tried to fill in for a short time. The real action started when my close friend and fellow speaker Campbell McAlpine came forward at the Holy Spirit's direction, and led the people in the application of the part of the message that had been taught.

He called for open confession and repentance where the fear of the Lord was not operating in the people's lives related to the teaching just given. For well over an hour there was a deep move of God's Spirit as one by one, leaders stood in genuine brokenness and contrition of heart, acknowledging before God and others their lack of the fear of the Lord and their desperate need to be changed. Many sought the face of God on their knees.

Only when we choose to be nothing can God be everything in any situation. Only when we truly fear God will we be released from the fear of people.

How many deep moves of God's Spirit have been missed in the Body of Christ because we've been insensitive or disobedient to the promptings of the Holy Spirit? My book published by Baker Books, entitled *Intimate Friendship With God: Through Understanding the Fear of the Lord,* gives full teaching on this important subject.

4. Unconditional obedience to God is the evidence of a holy life. In Joshua 24:14–18, Joshua called the Israelites to serve the Lord in sincerity and truth and to turn from all idolatry. He then gave his uncompromising declaration. "But as for me and my house, we will serve the LORD" (Joshua 24:15). The people's response sounded so spiritual. "Far be it from us that we should forsake the LORD to serve other gods" (Joshua 24:16). They recounted God's miraculous deliverances and preservations, and finished by stating, "We also will serve the LORD, for He is our God" (Joshua 24:18).

Joshua told them that they could not serve God like they were, because God is so much holier than their understanding of His holiness. Exactly the same scenario was repeated again, until finally the people said, "The LORD our God we will serve, and *His voice we will obey!*" (Joshua 24:24, emphasis added). Only then did Joshua make a covenant with the people, write down their commitment, and set up a large stone to remind them of what they'd said to God (see vv. 25–27).

What does all this tell us? We're only as "behaviorally holy" in God's sight as we are obedient to His voice.

In Numbers 15:37–40 we read that the Israelites made tassels on their garments with a blue cord attached, to remember the commandments of the Lord, in order to obey them, in order to be holy.

5. Unconditional obedience to God in action and motive is the evidence that we're living in the light of the judgment seat of Christ. We need to examine ourselves in the light of these solemn words:

- "You will be judged on whether or not you are doing what Christ wants you to. So watch what you do and what you think" (James 2:12 TLB).

- "So we make it our goal to please Him . . . for we must all appear before the judgment seat of Christ, that each one may receive what is due him for the things done while in the body, whether good or bad" (2 Corinthians 5:9–10 NIV).

- "The day will surely come when at God's command Jesus Christ will judge the secret lives of everyone, their inmost thoughts and motives . . ." (Romans 2:16 TLB).

A very healthy spiritual exercise is to frequently ask ourselves the following three questions.

- Am I doing what God has directed me to do?

- Is it in the timing that He has directed?

- Is it being done solely for God's glory, or is there some hidden motivation for self-promotion?

Then, we must wait on God long enough to receive the answers. He has them, and will disclose them to those who are diligent seekers and desperate for truth.

6. Unconditional obedience to God is also evidence that we qualify to be an overcomer, and that we are relating our lifestyle on earth in the light of the eons of time we'll spend in eternity. "To him who overcomes and *does My will to the end,* I will give authority over the nations" (Revelation 2:26 NIV, emphasis added). "*To him who overcomes* I will grant to sit with Me on My throne, as I also overcame and sat down with My Father on His throne. He who has an ear, let him hear what the Spirit says to the churches" (Revelation 3:21–22, emphasis added). Do you notice how conditional these promises are?

7. Unconditional obedience to God as a way of life is evidence of our being true disciples of the Lord Jesus Christ. I cannot stress too strongly the weighty implications of the Scripture verses I am going to share with you.

We must never be fooled into thinking that believing in the Lord Jesus Christ for salvation without a commitment of our wills to obey Him, will ever work in the Christian life, or gain eternal life. Listen to the unbridled facts of John 3:36:

He who believes in the Son has eternal life: he who does not obey the Son shall not see life, but the wrath of God rests upon him. (RSV)

God's Word makes it clear that we can only be sure that we are living in God, know Him, and have His love in us if we are obeying the truths from His Word.

Now by this we know that we know Him, if we keep His commandments. He who says, "I know Him," and does not keep His commandments, is a liar, and the truth is not in him. But whoever keeps His word, truly the love of God is perfected in him. By this we know that we are in Him. (1 John 2:3–5)

One day when Jesus was speaking to the multitudes, His mother and brothers stood outside the building trying to get His attention to speak with Him. When someone alerted Jesus to the need, He said that a close relationship with Him came only through obedience to Him, not through natural earthly ties.

And He stretched out His hand toward His disciples and said, "Here are My mother and My brothers! For whoever does the will of My Father in heaven is My brother and sister and mother." (Matthew 12:49–50)

The final thought-provoking verses are surely among the most grave and sobering verses in the Bible in relation to the outcome of many, not some, who will be convinced they are going to spend eternity in heaven, but in fact are not. Hell is the only alternative.

Not everyone who says to Me, "Lord, Lord," shall enter the kingdom of heaven, but he who *does the will of My Father* in heaven. Many will say to Me in that day, "Lord, Lord, have we not prophesied in Your name, cast out demons in Your name, and done many wonders in Your name?" And then I will declare to them, "I never knew you; depart from Me, you who practice lawlessness!" (Matthew 7:21–23, emphasis added)

The key to understanding these strong words is found in the last four words, "you who practice *lawlessness*" (emphasis added)—that means rebellion to authority. It means being untamed and uncontrolled, having no respect for commands and choosing to do our own thing. It means these people were supposedly serving God with vocal, spectacular ministries, giving lip service to the Lordship of Christ, but in fact were not under His Lordship at all. That's heavy-duty! The NIV renders verse 23: "Then I will tell them plainly, 'I never knew you. Away from Me, you evildoers!'"

I wonder how much more clearly God could warn us from His Word about the importance of unconditional obedience! Perhaps you are realizing how disobedient you are in areas of your life, or perhaps you are oblivious to areas of disobedience. The closing part of this section of the book is designed to help you. Please take it seriously.

Areas to Check with God Related to Obedience

Come before the Lord in stark honesty and invite the Holy Spirit to reveal to you any of the following areas where you may need to repent of disobedience.

Doing this spiritual exercise will help you to ascertain how serious you are in your relationships with God and others, and how your life lines up with issues that are important to God.

In Appendix C of this book, I have indicated where some of my teachings that relate to some of the following checklists are available.

1. Vocal worship and praise to God as a way of life

2. Intercession—have a daily prayer agenda for others

3. An effective time in the Word of God which produces a knowledge of God's character and ways

4. Witnessing as a way of life—Do you have a list of names of unconverted people for whom you regularly pray?

5. Eating and drinking habits—are they consistent with balanced nutrition?

6. Regular exercise

7. Family: (a) responsibilities, (b) relationships, (c) family worship

8. Finances: (a) tithes, (b) offerings, (c) pledges, (d) money owed to others

9. Letters, phone calls, and other forms of communication

10. Correction needed to give to others

11. Forgiveness

12. Expressed gratitude

13. Restitution—humbling to those we've wronged

14. Borrowed things that need to be returned

15. Obedience to the word of the Lord through messages we've heard, or been given personally by others in whom we trust

16. Things we have promised to do for others

17. Things God told us to give to others

18. Maintaining loving relationships at all times, based upon humility and the fear of the Lord

Who Is Your Role Model?

The Greatest Challenge, Opportunity, and Fulfillment

This section brings us to the heart of the message of this book. None of us can escape the challenge. Is the Lord Jesus really your mentor?

This question is the important issue at stake. Have we come to the place of revelation and commitment as a way of life to follow Jesus as our mentor? Before we answer too quickly, it is crucial to understand how He functioned in order for us to operate in the same way.

The earthly life of Jesus Christ stands unique in human history as the pattern for all Christians. We cannot afford to simply glance at it. We have to study it thoroughly from God's Word, understand it and apply the same principles to our lives.

We must spend time consistently alone with the Lord Jesus, worshiping Him, listening to His voice, and above all, obeying Him—only then do we get to be like Him, "but we all, with unveiled face, beholding as in a mirror the glory of the Lord, are being transformed into the same image from glory to glory, just as by the Spirit of the Lord" (2 Corinthians 3:18). "So I have looked for You in the sanctuary, to see Your power and Your glory" (Psalm 63:2).

How Did Jesus Function?

The Lord Jesus relinquished all rights to function as Son of God in order to fulfill the purpose of being sent to earth as

Son of Man. He laid aside His *function* of deity but retained His *nature* of deity.

He came to earth for a number of reasons, including:

- To show us what the Father is like. "The Son is the radiance of God's glory and the exact representation of His being . . ." (Hebrews 1:3 NIV).

- To seek and to save that which was lost (see Luke 19:10).

- To die upon the cross and make atonement for the sins of the world (see 1 Peter 3:18).

- To defeat the works of Satan (see 1 John 3:8).

- To show us how to live. "To this you were called, because Christ suffered for you, leaving you an example, that you should follow in His steps" (1 Peter 2:21 NIV). "He who says he abides in Him ought himself also to walk just as He walked" (1 John 2:6).

- To become our life. ". . . Christ in you, the hope of glory" (Colossians 1:27). "It is no longer I who live, but Christ lives in me; . . ." (Galatians 2:20).

For us to understand the importance of knowing and doing only the specific will of God at all times, we must look closely at Jesus. His life on earth was characterized by resoluteness and intensity of purpose to accomplish the task He had been given by the Father. "I have glorified You on the earth. I have finished the work which You have given Me to do" (John 17:4).

We need to keep checking in with God, asking Him to

show us where we may not be accomplishing God's will by not seeking Him enough to make sure we are the right person in the right place at the right time, saying and doing the right things with the right attitude of heart toward God and man. Believe me, that is time-consuming, but infinitely rewarding, as I trust you have discovered while reading this book.

How Jesus Related to the Father

Jesus' goal on earth was accomplished by the ultimate example of humility in the way He related to His Father, God. Our goal will only be accomplished as we relate to Him with the same kind of humility.

We often know instinctively from our upbringing or other training exactly what is the right thing to do, particularly regarding self-preservation. We know we must brush our teeth so they won't decay. We know we should look carefully to the right and left before crossing a street. These are nonnegotiable things. But circumstances often arise that require a weighed decision in matters large and small. There could be five good reasons why we should or should not take a certain course of action. And the more people that are involved in the outcome of our decisions, the greater our responsibility and accountability to God for our decisions to have come from hearing His voice.

Have you discovered that God does not bless our good ideas? There are a number of Scripture verses that talk about "the good and right thing." There can be several good things we could do, but there is only one right thing—the will of God. And that is when we need to follow Jesus' example of humility and seek God until we know for sure what He wants us to do.

- *Jesus related to the Father in absolute submission.* "For I have come down from heaven, not to do My own will, but the will of Him who sent Me" (John 6:38).

A public manifestation of this submission occurred when He was baptized in water and then empowered by the Holy Spirit before entering into public ministry.

> When all the people were baptized, it came to pass that Jesus also was baptized; and while He prayed, the heaven was opened. And the Holy Spirit descended in bodily form like a dove upon Him, and a voice came from heaven which said, "You are My beloved Son; in You I am well pleased." (Luke 3:21–22)

Water baptism, prayer, and being empowered by the Holy Spirit before entering public ministry were so important to Father God for His Son that He spoke His approval audibly from heaven. We can't afford to neglect any of these priorities.

The parallel challenge to us from Jesus' life of submission is, "And He died for all, that those who live should live no longer for themselves, but for Him who died for them and rose again" (2 Corinthians 5:15). What was important to Him must become important to us.

- *Jesus related to the Father in absolute dependence.*

Most assuredly, I say to you, the Son can do nothing of Himself, but what He sees the Father do; for whatever He does, the Son also does in like manner. (John 5:19)

I can of Myself do nothing. As I hear, I judge; and My judgment is righteous, because I do not seek My own will but the will of the Father who sent Me. (John 5:30)

- *Jesus sought to know the Father's will about everything.* He sought until He heard and understood. "I do nothing on My own but speak just what the Father has taught Me" (John 8:28 NIV). "I am telling you what I have seen in the Father's presence" (John 8:38 NIV).

- *Jesus related to the Father with absolute obedience.* ". . . I always do those things that please Him" (John 8:29).

For I have not spoken on My own authority; but the Father who sent Me gave Me a command, what I should say and what I should speak. And I know that His command is everlasting life. Therefore, whatever I speak, just as the Father has told Me, so I speak. (John 12:49–50)

- *Jesus related to the Father in absolute faith.* "Jesus said to them, 'My Father is always at His work to this very day, and I, too, am working'" (John 5:17 NIV). As a result of all this humility, Jesus never accepted praise from men, because the Father was the explanation of all that happened through the Son. He said, "Do you not believe that I am in the Father, and the Father in Me? The words that I speak to you I do not speak on My own authority; but the Father who dwells in Me does the works" (John 14:10).

Whenever people encourage us (and we should be giving encouragement to others as a way of life), it is of paramount importance that we consciously acknowledge to the Lord that He alone is the source of anything commendable in us and through us, and whenever possible, acknowledge it to others.

- *Jesus lived for His Father's glory.* "He who speaks from himself seeks his own glory; but He who seeks the glory of the One who sent Him is true, and no unrighteousness is in Him" (John 7:18).

- Jesus knew no presumptions. This produced coordination and total fulfillment. Therefore He knew no frustration!

How All This Teaching Affects Us Daily

All this teaching about how the Lord Jesus related to the Father when Jesus was on earth has everything to do with our everyday lives. Jesus prayed to the Father and said, "As You sent Me into the world, I also have sent them into the world" (John 17:18). Also, one of the last sentences Jesus spoke to His disciples before returning to the Father was, "Peace to you! As the Father has sent Me, I also send you" (John 20:21).

We are called of God to be representing the Lord Jesus as ambassadors in this world. If we are not choosing to live as

Jesus modeled for us, we are automatically presenting a distorted view of Him to others.

The only alternative lifestyle to living by these truths that Jesus exemplified is to revert to the pride that comes from saying and doing our own thing. And when we do, we should logically take the credit. We deserve it. Just don't be deceived into thinking anything spiritual happened! Jesus said, ". . . without Me you can do nothing" (John 15:5).

You can say and do your own thing as a missionary, pastor, Bible teacher, spiritual leader, dedicated and sacrificially living Christian. You can do it with zeal, fervor, eloquence, originality of thought, back it up with Scripture references, motivate people to follow you with enthusiasm and excitement, frequently ask God to bless your efforts, and never once function with spiritual authority.

What Is the Source of True Authority?

Spiritual authority is based solely on living by the same principles by which Jesus lived as the Son of Man. Everything He did was with authority, because it always had the Father's approval. He lived for the Father's glory. "I have glorified You on the earth. I have finished the work which You have given Me to do" (John 17:4). This brings us to the next vital question.

How Authentic Are We?

We are only as real, or as authentic a Christian, as we are when Jesus is the only explanation of our life, in the same way that the Father was the explanation of Jesus' life. Let's take a look at something that could have happened quite feasibly in Jesus' everyday life.

What would Jesus do if He was sitting in the synagogue and one of the rabbis was due to teach, but looked over and saw Jesus, and out of respect for Him, asked Him to come up and say something to the people first? This sort of thing happens frequently among Christians.

Jesus would only say what the Father told Him to say and He may have to wait for it. (It cost Jesus a whole night's sleep, seeking the Father before He could announce who His twelve apostles would be.) What do so many do when asked to say a few words unexpectedly to a group of people? You fill in the answer.

I attended a meeting in San Clemente, California, where the founder of a Bible college and conference center from the East Coast was the visiting speaker. Someone told him that I was in the audience, so just before he spoke he asked me to share, "whatever was on my heart." I had no prior notice.

I did not know the man knew me. I thanked him for asking me to share and explained that I had come with no other thought than to listen to him and learn from God. But I would seek God to see if He had anything to say through me. If He did, I would share; if not, I would have nothing to say. I asked him if that was okay with him, and he said, "Yes."

I waited on God in silence for several minutes, and then He spoke to me to share a few sentences on the truth that humility is one of our greatest needs in the body of Christ. I did so, and then prayed that God would release this revelation worldwide, believed for it, and returned to my seat.

The Deeper Implications of Pride and Unbelief

This teaching leaves us with the conclusion that to choose to live by any other standard than the one the Lord Jesus came to model for us, is preposterous pride. Proverbs 16:5 says that "everyone proud in heart is an abomination to the LORD."

One of the most prevalent forms of pride is manifest in the sin of presumption—through the lack of seeking God in detail. David, as a leader, cried out, "Keep back Your servant also from presumptuous sins; let them not have dominion over me. Then I shall be blameless, and I shall be innocent of *great transgression*" (Psalm 19:13, emphasis added).

Jesus, in His humility, modeled the total absence of this sin by only saying and doing what He saw and heard the Father say or do first. (See John 5:30; 12:49.)

God has been tolerating the private and public agendas in the lives of spiritual leaders and followers for a long time. I believe we are entering a time when God will increasingly manifest His disapproval of this form of pride. He may well embarrass us publicly in His love for us, to bring us to repentance. He did so with Jonah and Balaam. I used to say, "God will never embarrass you or overrule your free will." *Wrong.*

A young man in YWAM with strong leadership giftings was asked to speak to a group of Christians in another organization that he deeply respected. Without seeking God, he accepted the invitation and went with a message of his own choosing.

When his time to speak was announced, God brought him under such deep conviction of the sin of presumption that all he could do was to stand to his feet and tell them that he was never sent by God, therefore he had nothing to say. The leader of the group asked him if he would at least pray, and when the young leader tried, God temporarily paralyzed his tongue. He could not utter a single word, but only nod his head negatively.

The young leader had been thoroughly taught, in his training years, to wait on God before accepting any ministry assignment. If God confirmed he was to speak, he was then to wait on God for the exact word of the Lord in every situation. God knew the many thousands of people who would be influenced by his life and teaching in future days, and wanted to guard against the pride of presumption being perpetuated through his ministry. The Bible says, "He whom God has *sent* speaks the words of God" (John 3:34).

I have always been deeply grateful for the humility of that dear man of God for sharing that story with me out of his past experience. His openness and brokenness are being used of God to teach many the ways of the Spirit.

Then, there is the pride of wanting to control in group situations instead of having a listening ear to the Holy Spirit, who may want to sovereignly change the agenda. So often He is never given this prerogative. Sadly, the kind of story I'm now going to share with you is all too rare.

I will never forget the day a sensitive spiritual leader relinquished his control of a group he was leading, and made room for God. Jim and I were attending a YWAM Asian leadership conference in Hong Kong. One afternoon, the seven men who comprised the Asian leadership council sought God diligently, and in complete unity, received clear directions from the Holy Spirit as to God's purposes for the following day. That direction included my speaking to the conferees. The next day, I spoke from 9:00 A.M. until 10:00 A.M. on "Jesus, the Leader in Ministry." Immediately following, the chairman sensed a check in his spirit and said, "I believe we're to wait quietly on God and not pursue the rest of the agenda at this point."

After a few minutes of silence, God suddenly invaded that roomful of missionaries with one of the most awesome visitations of the Holy Spirit I have ever witnessed. The Holy Spirit alone took over and led the meeting without human instrumentality. It lasted for three hours. God's manifest presence came, by laying bare the hearts, as God only knows them to be, of many people in that room. Individuals spontaneously went forward one at a time to the pulpit and spoke with great brokenness and deep repentance about their areas of pride, unbelief, and resentment toward God—the kinds of sins to which we're blind until we see them in the light of God's white-hot holiness. One missionary from Scandinavia was literally wailing on her face on the floor, under deep conviction of sin for fifteen minutes as God showed her the spiritual pride in her heart because she was a missionary!

Another gifted Bible teacher had the sudden revelation that a message he had been teaching was rooted in the sin of unbelief and he would have to scrap it and never teach it again.

An Asian leader had the revelation that his concepts were warped both in relation to the character of God and in the way he related to other races and cultures. He sobbed his way through his repentance, asking forgiveness of those to whom this distortion of truth had affected.

It is mighty difficult to remain the same when God shows up with a revelation of His holiness that spotlights our unholiness. God does more in seconds and minutes when a cloudburst of the rain of the Spirit descends upon a group, than would normally take place in months or years of normal Christian activity, no matter how good.

I wonder how many life-changing moves of God's Spirit have been missed because leaders made sure they were in control! God is looking for those who will be prepared to leave their comfort and safety zones, choose to have the humility and faith to believe that "the government will be upon His shoulder[s]" (Isaiah 9:6). . . . and be super-sensitive to the restraints and constraints of the Holy Spirit.

Well, dear reader, having read everything in this book, you may be yearning to experience the adventure of hearing and obeying God's voice, but deep down inside your heart you're thinking, *It obviously works for others, but it won't work for me. The frequency of my failures to live the Christian life are all too numerous.*

But wait a minute. Admitting that you can't live the Christian life by your own effort is the starting point of the breakthrough for which you are longing.

I can't either. None of us can in our own strength, no matter how strong-willed we are. It takes Jesus Christ *in* us, to live like Jesus *through* us. Only as we daily tell Him that in ourselves we are bankrupt, that we desperately need Him to stand up in us and take over, and invite the Lord Jesus to live His life His way in us each day, and believe that He does, will anything spiritual happen in us and through us.

We simply need to agree with King David when he declared, "My goodness is nothing apart from You" (Psalm 16:2). We need to also agree with Jesus when He said, ". . . for without Me you can do nothing" (John 15:5). Nothing is zero. Zero is a circle with a hole in the middle. So that's who we are. The rim of each circle has a personal name above it for identification purposes. That's your name and mine and everyone else's. And we need to agree with Paul when he stated, "For I know that in me (that is, in my flesh) nothing good dwells; for to will is present with me, but how to perform what is good I do not find" (Romans 7:18). That's the bad news. The good news is *that all that we're not, Jesus is,* and that He lives within us. So let's look at the other side of the coin of truth.

"I can do all things through Christ who strengthens me" (Philippians 4:13). This verse gets even clearer when Paul explains,

> I have been crucified with Christ. My ego is no longer central. It is no longer important that I appear righteous before you or have your good opinion, and I am no longer driven to impress God. Christ lives in me. The life you see me living is not "mine," but it is lived by faith in the Son of God, who loved me and gave himself for me. (Galatians 2:20 THE MESSAGE)

We need to again agree with Paul when he states, ". . . Christ in you, the hope of glory" (Colossians 1:27). The "glory of God" is all of God's characteristics. Only God Himself can display those through us. Jesus Christ gave up His life for us on the cross, so that by His resurrected life, He could enter into the life of each one of us who receives Him and makes Him Lord. His intention and desire is to then live His life through us as we die to our own rights and desires. It's a fabulous exchange. It's a daily deal, where we invite the Lord Jesus who is within each one of us who are truly born again (see back Appendix A) to:

- think through our minds.
- look through our eyes.
- speak through our mouths.
- listen through our ears.
- love through our hearts.
- touch through our hands.
- walk through our feet.

Now, back to the circle with the hole in the middle (that's us). As we thank the Lord Jesus that He will do and is doing the above, His life goes into action, and the empty circle is filled with Him.

The beautiful person of the Holy Spirit within us will then prompt us if we have taken over from the Lord Jesus in any area of our lives. Through confession, repentance, and restitution, we allow Jesus to take full control again.

The Holy Spirit's empowerment enables us to keep the Lord Jesus on the throne of our hearts. That's why it is so important that we do not resist the Holy Spirit, grieve Him (see Ephesians 4:30), or quench Him (see 1 Thessalonians 5:19). Our safest place is to invite and believe for His total control (see Ephesians 5:18) ". . . the Holy Spirit whom God has given to those who obey Him" (Acts 5:32).

When we understand that Jesus Christ lives His life through us as we are daily under His lordship, and empowered by the Holy Spirit, the sweat is taken out of living and the striving stops. Before doing anything God has shown us to do, we simply say, "I can't, but You can and will. Now, thank You." That's what I call the miracle takeover! The Bible calls it "the rest of faith" (see Hebrews 4).

Now, who alone must logically get all the glory from the spiritual things that take place in us and through us? Certainly not us! We're only a rim surrounding a hole! This makes it so liberating and wonderfully easy to give all the glory, all the time to the only One worthy to receive it—King God, the Lover of our souls. "For of Him and through Him and to Him are all things, to whom be glory forever. Amen" (Romans 11:36).

Now, you and I have no excuse other than to either start or continue on the most fulfilling adventure of hearing and obeying God's voice. For everyone who reads this book, I have fervently prayed the following prayers in faith:

". . . that you may be filled with the knowledge of His will in all wisdom and spiritual understanding; that You may walk worthy of the Lord, fully pleasing Him, being fruitful in every good work and increasing in the knowledge of God" (Colossians 1:9–10).

". . . that you may stand perfect and complete in all the will of God" (Colossians 4:12).

And that you will be Forever Ruined for the Ordinary.

Dear Reader,

Because this is a book related to divine guidance, I understand that there may be people who would want to write to me requesting that I seek God on their behalf for answers to their questions, or get confirmation on their impressions. Please understand that there is no way that I can fulfill that expectation.

Firstly, the whole purpose of this book is to help you develop a relationship with the Lord whereby you hear God's voice for yourself. Your dependency on the Lord Himself needs to be increased, and this purpose would be defeated by my trying to get answers from God for you.

Secondly, it is impossible for me to cope with the correspondence that accompanies that sort of request and fulfill God's priorities for my life.

I am already inundated with correspondence and need less, not more. Thank you for your cooperation.

Very sincerely and warmly,

JOY DAWSON

What It Means to Commit Your Life to the Lord Jesus Christ

... Choose for yourselves this day whom you will serve ... as for me ... [I] will serve the LORD. (Joshua 24:15)

And He made from one every nation of men to live on all the face of the earth, having determined allotted periods and the boundaries of their habitation, that they should seek God, in the hope that they might feel after Him and find Him. Yet He is not far from each one of us. (Acts 17:26–27 RSV)

1. Acknowledge that you are a sinner and repent of your sin.

   For all have sinned and fall short of the glory of God. (Romans 3:23)

Repent therefore and be converted, that your sins may be blotted out. . . (Acts 3:19)

If we confess our sins, He is faithful and just to forgive us our sins and to cleanse us from all unrighteousness. (1 John 1:9)

2. Believe Christ died and rose again to save you from your sin and to give you eternal life.

For Christ died for sins once for all, the righteous for the unrighteous, to bring you to God. (1 Peter 3:18 NIV)

For there is one God and one Mediator between God and men, the Man Christ Jesus. (1 Timothy 2:5)

For God so loved the world that He gave His only begotten Son, that whoever believes in Him should not perish but have everlasting life. (John 3:16)

Nor is there salvation in any other, for there is no other name under heaven given among men by which we must be saved. (Acts 4:12)

3. Receive Christ by faith and accept the gift God has provided in His Son.

Jesus said to him, "I am the way, the truth, and the life. No one comes to the Father, except through Me." (John 14:6)

Yet to all who received him, to those who believed in his name, he gave the right to become children of God. (John 1:12 NIV)

Behold, I stand at the door and knock. If anyone hears My voice and opens the door, I will come in . . . (Revelation 3:20)

. . . God has given us eternal life, and this life is in His Son. He who has the Son has life; he who does not have the Son of God does not have life. (1 John 5:11–12)

4. Commit your whole life to the Lord Jesus Christ and follow Him and serve Him without reserve.

Whoever believes in the Son has eternal life; but whoever rejects the Son will not see life, for God's wrath remains on him. (John 3:36 NIV)

. . . If anyone desires to come after Me, let him deny himself, and take up his cross, and follow Me. (Matthew 16:24)

Anyone who loves his father or mother more than Me is not worthy of Me; anyone who loves his son or daughter more than Me is not worthy of Me; and anyone who does not take his cross and follow Me is not worthy of Me. (Matthew 10:37–38 NIV)

So He said to them, "Assuredly, I say to you, there is no one who has left house or parents or brothers or wife or children, for the sake of the kingdom of God, who shall not receive many times more in this present time, and in the age to come eternal life." (Luke 18:29–30)

5. Be prepared to confess Christ and to tell others that you belong to Him.

. . . If you confess with your lips that Jesus is Lord and believe in your heart that God raised him from the dead, you will be saved. For man believes with his heart and so is justified, and he confesses with his lips and so is saved. (Romans 10:9–10 RSV)

Therefore whoever confesses Me before men, him I will also confess before My Father who is in heaven. But whoever denies Me before men, him I will also deny before My Father who is in heaven. (Matthew 10:32–33)

For whoever is ashamed of Me and My words, of him the Son of Man will be ashamed when He comes in His own glory, and in His Father's, and of the holy angels. (Luke 9:26)

6. Acknowledge that the Lord Jesus not only died upon the Cross to give you eternal life, but that He rose again from the dead to live His life in you and through you.

. . . Christ in you, the hope of glory. (Colossians 1:27)

I have been crucified with Christ and I no longer live, but Christ lives in me. The life I live in the body, I live by faith

in the Son of God, who loved me and gave Himself for me.
(Galatians 2:20 NIV)

Your prayer of commitment of your life to the Lord Jesus Christ:

Lord Jesus, I know that I am a sinner. I turn away from my sin, in repentance, and ask You to forgive me. I believe You died on the cross for my sin and I thank You with all my heart. I now invite You to come into my heart and life. By faith, I receive You as my Savior, and make You my Lord and Master. I place my whole life in Your hands without reserve. Thank You that You not only died to give me the gift of eternal life, but that You rose again to live Your life in me and through me. I am prepared to acknowledge You as my Lord before others, and in constant dependence upon the Holy Spirit live for You, in obedience to Your promptings. Thank You that according to Your Word You have come in and made me Your child. Thank You that You have cleansed and forgiven me for my sin, and have given me eternal life.

Appendix B

Essentials for Progress as a Christian

1. Daily prayer and reading of God's Word are absolutely essential for you to grow strong spiritually.

You could start by reading the Gospel of John and the Psalms. Ask God the Holy Spirit to give you understanding and then thank Him that He will.

> But without faith it is impossible to please Him, for he who comes to God must believe that He is, and that He is a rewarder of those who diligently seek Him. (Hebrews 11:6)

Underline a verse when God speaks to you from it. The Bible is your guide and map.

> Your word is a lamp to my feet
> And a light to my path. (Psalm 119:105)

Do not confine prayers to "asking," but include thanksgiving and praise.

> . . . With thanksgiving, let your requests be made known to God. (Philippians 4:6)

> Praise Him for His acts of power;
> Praise Him for His surpassing greatness! (Psalm 150:2 NIV)

2. Seek God's guidance in all things and expect Him to give it.

> I will instruct you and teach you in the way you should go;
> I will counsel you and watch over you. (Psalm 32:8 NIV)

> He has promised to speak to us.

> My sheep hear My voice, and I know them, and they follow Me. (John 10:27 RSV)

3. Meet regularly with other keen Christians in the church fellowship to which God leads you.

> They devoted themselves to the apostles' teaching and to the fellowship, to the breaking of bread and to prayer. (Acts 2:42 NIV)

> Let us not give up meeting together, as some are in the habit of doing, but let us encourage one another—and all the more as you see the Day approaching. (Hebrews 10:25 NIV)

4. An important method of public witness is to experience believer's baptism.

> And as they went along the road they came to some water, and the eunuch said, "See, here is water! What is to prevent my being baptized?" (Acts 8:36 RSV)

By baptism we make an open confession of our faith in the Lord Jesus Christ in the way in which He commanded us.

> Go therefore and make disciples of all the nations, baptizing them in the name of the Father and of the Son and of the Holy Spirit. (Matthew 28:19)

5. Seek opportunities to lead others to Christ.

> . . . He who wins souls is wise. (Proverbs 11:30 NIV)

> "Come, follow Me," Jesus said "and I will make you fishers of men." (Matthew 4:19 NIV)

6. Remember that your enemy, the devil, and his demons will attack you in many ways, trying to make you sin.
James 4:7 says:

> "Therefore submit to God. Resist the devil and he will flee from you."

> Say, "It is written: 'Greater is he [the Lord Jesus Christ] that is in [me], than he [the devil] that is in the world.'" (1 John 4:4 KJV)

7. Should you fall into sin, do not be discouraged, but in repentance confess all to the Lord.

. . . Let everyone who names the name of Christ depart from iniquity. (2 Timothy 2:19)

8. . . . Be filled with the Spirit (Ephesians 5:18).

God the Holy Spirit is a Person who wants to completely control your life, so that the Lord Jesus Christ may be made real to you, and then through you to others.

Without His control you will be a powerless, ineffective Christian.

• Surrender your will totally to God.

. . . the Holy Spirit whom God has given to those who obey Him. (Acts 5:32)

• Be thorough in confession and repentance of all known sin.

He who covers his sins will not prosper,
But whoever confesses and forsakes them will have mercy.
(Proverbs 28:13)

• Ask God to fill you with His Spirit.

If you then, being evil, know how to give good gifts to your children, how much more will your heavenly Father give the Holy Spirit to those who ask Him! (Luke 11:13)

- Believe that He will, and thank Him for doing so.

. . . For whatever is not from faith is sin. (Romans 14:23)

Allow the Holy Spirit to manifest Himself in whatever way He chooses, by being obedient to His promptings.

These conditions need to be fulfilled constantly in order to maintain the Spirit-filled life.

Appendix C

Additional Resources Related to Obedience at the End of Section 6

All of Joy Dawson's resources are available from:

> YWAM
> 11141 Osborne St.
> Lake View Terrace, CA 91342, USA

1. Vocal worship and praise to God as a way of life (tapes: JD-40; JD-27)

2. Intercession—having a daily prayer agenda for others (see my book: *Intercession, Thrilling and Fulfilling*, YWAM Publishing, chapter 19)

3. Effective time in the Word of God, which produces a knowledge of God's character and ways (tapes: JD-53; JD-54)

4. Witnessing and praying for the unconverted as a way of life (tapes: JD-145; JD-72a; JD-72b; JD-74)

5. Eating habits (see my book: *Some of the Ways of God in Healing*, YWAM Publishing, chapter 9)

6. Regular exercise

7. Family responsibilities, family relationships, and family worship (tape: JD-67)

8. Finances: tithes, offerings, pledges, money owed to others (tape JD-86)

9. Letters, phone calls, or other communication

10. Needing to give correction to others (tapes: JD-65; JD-69)

11. Forgiveness (tape: JD-64)

12. Expressing gratitude

13. Making restitution: humbling ourselves before those we have wronged (tapes: JD-38; JD-25)

14. Returning things we have borrowed

15. Walking in obedience to the word of the Lord through messages we have heard, or ones given personally by others in whom we trust

16. Being faithful to keep our word when we've made promises to others

17. Being obedient to give to God and others when He directs (tapes: JD-95-96; JD-97 A, B, C)

18. Maintaining loving relationships at all times, based on humility and the fear of the Lord (tape: JD-6)

The Lydia Fellowship has excellent printed material on the subject of Scripture meditation. It is available from them at the following address:

> Lydia Fellowship
> P.O. Box 4509
> Mountain View, CA 94040-9996, USA
> www.lydiafellowship.org

Free Catalog

Hear Joy Dawson teach on almost 200 different key subjects.

Ideal for: Training Schools, Bible Institutes, churches, home groups, private study

Resource Guide
with many new additions

LIFE CHANGING
BOOKS • VIDEOTAPES
AUDIOTAPES

By Joy Dawson

For many years Joy Dawson has ministered extensively around the world as a Bible teacher and conference speaker, and has authored a number of books. Her penetrating teachings are based upon the character and ways of God. Multitudes have found them to be life changing. Her missionary journeys have taken her to fifty five nations. Joy and her husband Jim, along with their two married children and six grandchildren are with Youth With A Mission. They all live in Los Angeles.

Youth With A Mission

11141 Osborne St. • Lake View Terrace, CA 91342
Phone: (818) 896-2755 • Fax: (818) 897-6738

Send your name
and address to:

Youth With a Mission
11141 Osborne Street
Lake View Terrace, CA 91342, U.S.A.
Phone: (818) 896-2755
Fax: (818) 897-6738

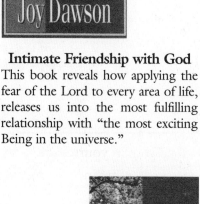

Some of the Ways in Healing

Joy is ruthless in her pursuit of truth on the subject of healing. Truth itself heals. All-out integrity in the probing of Scripture on the subject.

Intimate Friendship with God

This book reveals how applying the fear of the Lord to every area of life, releases us into the most fulfilling relationship with "the most exciting Being in the universe."

The Character of the One Who Says "Go"

This booklet deals with aspects of God's character that make us secure in Him when we obey the Great Commission of Mark 16:15.

How to Pray for Someone Near You Who is Away from God

Powerful insights in prayer that cause God's hand to be moved on behalf of others.

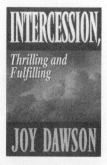

Intercession, Thrilling and Fulfilling

- Do you desire rapid spiritual growth?
- Do you want to enter a deeper dimension of effective ministry without leaving home?
- Do you long to be involved in a ministry that shapes nations?
- Do you want to be free from the guilt of prayerlessness— permanently.
- Are you ready to be inspired, stretched, and changed?

When the truths in this book are applied, these desires will be fulfilled; you will be ruined for the ordinary and never again think prayer is dull.

Dear Reader,

Because this is a book related to divine guidance, I understand that there may be people who would want to write to me requesting that I seek God on their behalf for answers to their questions, or get confirmation on their impressions. Please understand that there is no way that I can fulfill that expectation.

Firstly, the whole purpose of this book is to help you develop a relationship with the Lord whereby you hear God's voice for yourself. Your dependency on the Lord Himself needs to be increased, and this purpose would be defeated by my trying to get answers from God for you.

Secondly, it is impossible for me to cope with the correspondence that accompanies that sort of request and fulfill God's priorities for my life.

I am already inundated with correspondence and need less, not more. Thank you for your cooperation.

Very sincerely and warmly,

JOY DAWSON